Daily Scoldings

A Bracing Tonic
of Criticism, Rebuke,
and Punitive Inspiration
for Better Living

by Beryl Barclay

Illustrations by Stephen Jones

RUNNING PRESS
PHILADELPHIA · LONDON

9   8   7   6   5   4   3   2   1
Digit on the right indicates the number of this printing

Library of Congress Control Number: 2010930211

ISBN 978-0-7624-3806-8

Cover and interior design by Bill Jones
Illustrations by Stephen Jones
Edited by Jennifer Kasius
Typography: Bembo and Harrington

Running Press Book Publishers
2300 Chestnut Street
Philadelphia, PA 19103-4371

Visit us on the web!
www.runningpress.com

For Ted Fujioka.

Thanks to all the Andersons and Joneses—

especially Jon, Elaine, Neil, Dana, Stephen, and

Glenn—and Jennifer Kasius, Jane Lowe,

and Kathy Estell.

—B. B.

For Laura, Quinn, and Isabelle.

—S. J.

My Dear Readers:

Trying to make yourself feel better always makes you feel worse. Why? Because you are a contrarian. "No, I am not," you insist. Do you see? Each time you say, "I am a good person," you strengthen your rebuttal reflex, which responds, "No, I am not." Do not provoke your inner contrarian with cheerful self-talk. You are lying to yourself with each recitation of so-called affirmation, and you know it. Thus, you despise yourself all the more. It is worse, however, if by some psychological calamity you adore yourself above all else. Do not feed your narcissism, my darlings. Narcissism is a voracious beast. It will steal food out of the mouths of infants. It must be kept on a restricted diet of crabgrass and thorns. As a curative for rampant despair and narcissism, I offer this humble volume of scolding. My fondest wish is to slap you upside the head six ways till Sunday. This is my gift to you.

Bold Beginnings Are Bluster

You swear you're going to transform yourself. Improve yourself. Fix yourself. Never has your resolve been stronger. You intend to start anew, blazing and determined. My darlings, this is no way to begin anything of consequence. The times cry out for a roaring bonfire. To make a bonfire, first you must light the kindling. All it takes is a spark or two. For now, be content with striking the flint. You're building a fire that must burn through a long, cold night in the wilderness. Once it catches, the light and heat will be hard to extinguish. Be patient. Do not get ahead of yourself with a blowtorch and chemical accelerants. Indeed, they ruin the simple poetry of my metaphor.

Fuel for the Fire

You are not living up to your potential. You wallow in ignorance. You waste what is valuable. You fail your fellows at every turn. Suffering, greed, resentment, and confusion are the hallmarks of your existence. You are trapped in a prison of cowardice. Don't expect me to cater to your moods. Any sparks yet?

Recognize the Five Obvious Facts

1. You will die. You most certainly will.

2. Happiness is not life's purpose, but it is possible.

3. Others will disappoint you; but mostly, you will disappoint yourself.

4. Some people are utterly without conscience. You must learn to deal with them.

5. Life is worth living, regardless.

This Is Not a Dress Rehearsal

At some point, you have to understand that this is your life. I mean this. Right here. Now. This is it. You can't keep projecting a fantasy future. You can't keep delaying, telling yourself you'll be happy when your job, relationship, health, whatever improves. You have to live your life, right now. You're waiting for circumstances to be perfect. But they'll never be perfect. Perfection is a fiction, a story you tell yourself. If you want to change everything, change this story. Get rid of the fairy princesses and dragons, and look at the cast of characters around you. You mean something to them, and they to you. Show up. Figure it out. Stop running away.

Dread Is the Great Motivator

A re you anxious? Do you feel naked fear? Use your fear as an inspiration. When you open your mail and see exorbitant bills you can't pay, get inspired. Don't panic. Fight. Are you sweating buckets? How auspicious. How inspiring. You need a little desperation to put color in your cheeks.

JANUARY 6

Don't Fixate on Yourself So Much

Some people say, "I am brilliant." Or, "I am sexy hot." They take pride in these things and look down on others who are not as sexy hot, perhaps. Other people say, "I am a bastard." Or, "I am hideous." These thoughts can become a vicious self-fulfilling prophecy. Hideous bastards, you know it's true. Don't get too attached to what you think of yourself. It will change.

Just to Be Clear

I'm not the fixer of everything that's wrong in your life. I'm not responsible for your every bruise and scrape. I'm not your own personal cheerleading squad. I have a life, too. I have my own problems. Your expectation that my job is to somehow salve your childhood wounds and redeem your professional disappointments is wildly unrealistic. It puts an enormous strain on our relationship.

You're Not Winning Any Prizes for Empathy

You fret over your appearance, your accomplishments, and your status in the world. You want everyone to regard you positively. If they did, then maybe you could feel good about yourself. But people are too concerned about their own appearance, accomplishments, and status to pay much attention to you. Learn to bask in the indifference of others. Enjoy their lack of insight. You don't understand them, either.

Indolence Perpetuates Itself

Our worst fear is not that we are powerful beyond measure. Our worst fear is that hard work is required of us. We don't spend the day eating snacks on the couch because we're terrified of success. We do it because it's comfortable, and we have unlimited access to television crime-drama programming. Get cracking.

The Story of Procrastinating Max

A beaver named Max lived in a clear mountain stream. He played in the water during the summer and sunned himself on the riverbank well into autumn. When the first frost set in, his friends urged him to put a fresh coat of mud on his lodge to protect him during the harsh winter, which would soon be upon them. Instead, Max lazed away the days. His lodge remained in disrepair. Bitter cold swept down from the mountains. Shivering and miserable in his leaky lodge, Max vowed that as soon as summer returned, he would fix his roof. But he did not get the chance. A wolverine tore through the roof and ate poor Max. Wolverines are notorious for exploiting weakness. Nature is cruel. Don't cry about Max. Fix your roof.

Do Not Feed the Bears

Unlimited joyful awareness resides in you somewhere. If you sit quietly, it will begin to show itself. Imagine that you're in the woods, sitting on a big rock. If you remain very still and quiet for a long time, you will see animals go about their business while paying no attention to you. Deer and bears unaware of your presence will wander past you. Likewise, your joy will emerge when you become still. So, hush. Bears turn nasty when startled. Also, they will rip you to shreds if they smell food on you. Relax as if your life depends on it.

Lace Up Your Boots

A river follows the path of least resistance, and so it becomes crooked. People are like this, too. If you habitually wind and weave your way around obstacles, your path eventually departs from the straight and true. If you encounter a giant boulder in your path, it's there for your benefit. You can become strong by climbing over it, rather than become sneaky by skirting it. Sometimes humble prayer can roll a stone away. But you should plan on a difficult climb.

Who Are You Fooling?

A well-meaning guru once advised, "Fake it till you make it." If you don't feel sincere or confident, you should pretend that you do until you acquire sincerity and confidence. I have another name for this technique. I call it "fooling yourself." I don't recommend it. Self-deception is the nature of your problem, not the cure.

JANUARY 14

Avoid Prison If Possible

There is no comfort to be gained from inflicting suffering upon others. Criminal conduct is always out of the question. Yes, in most states, spiking your spouse's food with laxatives is rightly a criminal offense. No matter how bad you feel now, going to jail will make you feel worse. Incarceration is extremely awkward and confining.

JANUARY 15

A Caution Regarding Vengeance

Revenge does not "get even" with anyone. Rather, it perpetuates suffering. I cannot endorse the seeking of revenge. No matter how righteous you feel, any attempt to harm another will inevitably rebound upon you. How do you think I got this gimpy leg?

JANUARY 16

Be the Bigger Person

What shall you do about your lying, cheating spouse? My darling, you must banish all thoughts of reunion or revenge. Hold your head high. Walk away. Do not look back. After all, your spouse and I truly love each other. We've booked a cruise. Let the healing begin.

JANUARY 17

No Use in Stewing

Dwell for a moment on all beings who have thwarted your pursuit of important life goals. Your tyrannical boss. Your shallow romantic interest who could not appreciate the "real you." Your two-faced gossiping friend. Think of how they have hurt you. Can you feel your heart clench? You will give yourself a heart attack. Don't give your enemies the satisfaction.

Not All Wild Elephants Can Be Tamed

O nce upon a time, a wild elephant went on a rampage and damaged many mobile homes in Michigan. A woman sought to tame the elephant by singing sweetly to it. The elephant was calmed by the lullaby and fell fast asleep. The woman felt sympathy and kindness for the great beast, even though it had created havoc. Soon, the woman fell asleep, too. When she awoke, she found the elephant baking brownies. Everyone was sad when they learned there were warrants out for the elephant's arrest on drug and weapons charges. It seemed like such a nice elephant, once you got to know it. Great sages teach that an untamed mind is more dangerous than a wild elephant. Culturally speaking, wild elephants do not rank on our list of potential threats. But if they were high on meth and suspected of selling uranium to terrorists, we might rightly grow concerned.

You Underestimate the Peril of Your Situation

I have endured a long and bitter life. I have tasted joy and sorrow. You may resist what I tell you as defiant children resist good sense. You may spit it out like foul-tasting medicine. It is medicine nonetheless. You are wrapped in petty pleasure or trapped in seemingly inescapable pain. You are sleepwalking. Worse, you are sleep-eating, sleep-driving, and sleep-talking on your cell phone, all at the same time. Wakey wakey.

Wake Up "Big Roxy"

We each embody a clear, dazzling nature, which some call God, Buddha, Divinity, or Big Roxy Macallan. We all have it whether we are smart or stupid, fat or thin, married or single. We are all equal in this way. If you believe you must go to college or get a promotion or have plastic surgery before you can reveal your Big Roxy Macallan, you are mistaken. Roxy is happy to play with you just as you are.

Let's Agree

Do not kiss my buttocks. I will not kiss yours. This is a good rule of thumb for negotiating in the modern world, and it may slow the spread of infectious disease.

The Tragic Irony

No one gives a crap about how you feel about yourself, why you failed yesterday, and the great things you hope to accomplish tomorrow. No one cares—except for the long-suffering person who loves you most. Usually, this is the one person with whom you cannot be bothered, the one whom you take for granted. You revere holy texts, horoscopes, and fortune-cookie sayings. But wisdom spoken to you by your own dearest auntie goes in one ear and out the other. Sniffle.

Sorry Seems to Be the Weakest Word

Suppose you have done something ghastly, whether knowingly or unknowingly. Suppose you have tortured kittens. Suppose you have murdered villages. What do you say? *Sorry?* You bear guilt that cannot be pardoned. You cannot hope to be released from this weight through ritual or prayer. Rather, you must bear it and become strong enough to carry it with you always as a reminder of what you have been and what you choose to no longer be. I forgive you, but that doesn't absolve you of anything.

Insecurity
Makes No Sense

It pains me when a person I love thinks his or her body is less than beautiful. So-called imperfections are exactly what I love. But when I assert this, I am met with scoffing. When I am told the same thing in response to my own insecurity, I scoff too. Insecurity is perplexing. If you are unhappy with your appearance, try to imagine what you will look like when you are dead and moldering. By comparison, you look fabulous.

Losers and More Losers

If you delight in the misfortune of others, you are a loser. I am not saying this to be hurtful. I am saying it so you will challenge your attitude of entitlement and self-importance. A winner in life is someone who wants everyone to win, not just oneself. If the only way you can win is by holding someone else down, you are a loser. You may be the most winning player in the history of your chosen sport, but if your life is ruled by your schlong, you are a loser. If you exaggerate other people's flaws and go around trumpeting to everyone that so-and-so is a loser because he did such-and-such thing with his schlong, you are a loser, too.

Inherent in Every Problem Is Its Solution

People come to me with their problems. I don't provide answers. I provide questions. The solutions to most of our problems can be coaxed from our unconscious through riddles and queries. For example, a woman came to me in grave distress. She said, "For the past year my husband has been suffering from the delusion that he is an airplane." I asked why she hadn't sought help sooner. She replied, "Because it has been so nice to fly for free whenever we want." A simple case of codependency. I gave her some motion sickness pills and sent her on her way.

JANUARY 27

Three Rules

The Golden Rule can be summed up as, "Treat others as you would have them treat you." Related to the Golden Rule is the so-called Silver Rule, which states the same idea in negative terms: "Do not do to others what you do not want others to do to you." I'm lobbying for ratification of a Bronze Rule: "Maintain one car length behind the car in front of you for every ten miles-per-hour of speed." Most people are unaware of this dictum. When you tailgate, honk, or flash your lights in my rearview mirror, you're completely out of medal contention.

Pondering the Complexity of Humor

Some say that humor is a mechanism for coping with pain. If this is true, you can cheer yourself with the thought that you have given your loved ones much to laugh about. Others say that humor is a form of aggression. If this is true, I'd much rather be hit over the head with a joke than a brickbat, wouldn't you? Still others say that humor results when we perceive incongruity. When, for instance, there is a buildup of expectation, and suddenly you are confronted with something you had not anticipated. If this is true, you'll expect a punch line here. Generally, if you can't find something gentle and humane to laugh about, twink off.

Phallic Jocularity

A m I alone in lamenting the decline of humor? I'm stunned by the proliferation of penis jokes, for example. I find nothing inherently hilarious about the human penis. During our brief dalliance, Millard Fillmore once attired his member with a miniature ascot and vest. A marvelous ventriloquist, he recited portions of his state-of-the-union speech in the high-pitched voice of Little Filly. Millard was a forgettable president, but Filly was a scream. My point is that penis jokes are amusing only if the penis in question has a flair for comedy.

Benefits of Mastication

When all else fails, chew a piece of gum. Chewing gum boosts blood flow to the brain and stimulates the cranial nerves. You'll be able to think more clearly. Increased saliva and a strong dose of mint will take the edge off your breath. You're wilting my roses. No smacking, cracking, or bubble blowing in company, please.

Three Dicta
Pertaining to Monkeys

1. Do not poke a caged monkey with a stick lest it fling poo in your face.

2. Do not poke a caged monkey with a stick lest it die unexpectedly of an unrelated, preexisting condition. You will be blamed.

3. Do not poke a caged monkey with a stick. Such senseless cruelty is pitiful. There is nothing worse for your self-esteem than being pitied by a caged monkey.

Purge Something Useless

Traditionally, February is the month of purgation. The word "February," which comes to us from distant Roman origins, literally means purification. I suspect the word "fever" grows from the same root. This is a time to burn, sweat, pine, weep, and purge the toxic sludge from your soul, dribbling out a triumphant puddle of goo, so you can get on with your life. It's unpleasant, but you'll look several ounces lighter by March. Do you really need to drag all your resentments around with you like a bag of bricks?

You Cannot Purge Darkness

You tell yourself: if I could rid myself of everything bad, wrong, or undesired, all would be well. This is an error. You can never purge darkness from yourself, even with your fingers down your throat. No, what you must purge instead is the denial of your own darkness. "Darkness?" you may scoff. "What darkness?" Indeed. The dreary month of February will show you the cold, hard lack of empathy within. This is the grim purgatory between the bold beginning of the year and the distant promise of spring. Lucky for you, it's a short month.

Rudeness Multiplies Rudeness

Trying to fight rudeness with rudeness is like arguing with a mirror reflection, or trying to get away from your own shadow on the pavement. Most people behave poorly. Behaving poorly in retaliation only makes matters worse. Patience and forbearance are much more effective, more shocking and provocative. It's dumbfounding when a person behaves well. You can't even imagine yourself treating boors with kindness, can you? That's how novel it is.

The Demise of Whole Empires

Once upon a time, rudeness was ironic. Disrespect had meaning as a counterpoint to respect. There's no respect anymore. Rudeness is no longer playfully transgressive. There's nothing left to transgress. Soon, the pendulum will swing the other way, and good manners will seem daring and brash. That is, unless our society dissolves into anarchy and civil war, which is likely if people keep talking on their cell phones while simultaneously speaking with shop clerks.

Get Worked Up about Something Consequential

My, aren't we a privileged bunch that we can squander our outrage on telemarketers, loud talkers, and serial belchers. We howl about the slights, oversights, and inconveniences perpetrated against us by insensitive, ill-mannered people. How petty. How childish. On the bright side, we have no real problems. If the worst thing that happens to you today is hearing music from someone else's car stereo, revel in your pampered life and shut your yap.

Unmistakable Fragrance

It is said that a flower perfumes the hand that gives it. Likewise, one who gives crap retains a whiff of scent.

FEBRUARY 7

A Gift of Crap

If someone offers you a pile of steaming crap and you refuse to accept it, what happens to it? Who owns it? "I'm not taking your crap," you might say. "Well, it's not my crap anymore," the giver might reply. The crap has been disowned. But it persists, presenting a risk to public health, threatening to contaminate water supplies with its bacteria and putrefaction. Someone must deal with the crap before it kills us all. What are you doing this afternoon that could possibly be more important?

Are You a Crap Filter?

In my day, dealing with disowned crap was the job of the municipal government. Now, City Hall is up to its neck in it. Many people are incapable of dealing with their own crap. They're incapable of accepting blame or responsibility. Everything is someone else's fault, someone else's problem. Thankfully, some people have an uncanny ability to collect and neutralize the crap of others. Blessed are the crap filters. They spend weeks and years of emotional energy processing other people's crap. Often, they wake up depressed and wonder why. They're dealing with disowned crap, that's why.

Karma Is Beyond Your Ken

If karma were a simple formula of doing right and, in return, reaping reward, the world would be ruled by kindness. It's not. Karma is not a cumulative award program in which you accrue frequent flyer miles. Put all thoughts of gain or acquisition out of your mind. It is impossible to fathom one's karma, let alone cynically manipulate it. You are in freefall with nothing to hold on to. Everything you cherish will end with a splat, you know not when. Have some humility.

Always the Right Time to Begin

Some people need the incipient energy of the New Year to motivate them. They want a fresh start. These are people who insist on beginning things on Mondays or on the first of the month. Starting something on the tenth seems inauspicious. If you are one of these people, get a grip on yourself. Dates are completely arbitrary. Among the Chinese, Tibetans, Celts, and ancient Mayans, you'll find a host of different dates designated as new beginnings. Every day is someone's New Year. Don't be a slave to the calendar.

FEBRUARY 11

It Could Be Worse

Romans and other pagans of yore had such rot-
ten luck with romance that they resorted to
drawing names out of a basket. Single men would
pick from one basket, and single women would
choose from another. These pairings would last for
one year, until the next annual fertility festival. Stop
complaining about online dating. You have it easy.

FEBRUARY 12

All Lovers Are Stealthy Ninjas

If you don't have a lover, it's a problem. If you do
have a lover, it's another kind of problem. Lovers
don't solve problems. Rather, they add layers of
complication and difficulty whether they are absent
or present. Don't kid yourself. All lovers are unpre-
dictable shadow-warriors capable of snapping your
soul like a matchstick.

Human Beings Versus Sex Toys

Humans are not sex-service dispensers, even if you are paying them to act like sex-service dispensers. If you cannot recognize the humanity, independence, vulnerability, strength, and beauty of the person you're having sex with, you do not deserve to have sex with a human being. Back to sex toys for you. Sex toys are not people. They are appropriate objects of selfish gratification and kinky lust. They will not sass you. Many are dishwasher safe. But they don't provide companionship or remember your birthday, now, do they?

A Crucial Question

You may well ask yourself: When will I find a lover who is the wings on my back instead of the stone around my neck? You may well ask, for your lover is asking the same question.

Value of a Spouse

Procreation and economic stability aside, spouses serve a valuable function. One's spouse is one's personal representative for all humankind. A spouse looks closely and critically at you and your situation. He or she validates or rebuts your perceptions. He or she tells you how others at the party really perceive you. Your spouse is your ambassador, translating the world for you so you can have a clue. You serve the same function in turn for your spouse. When you look at it this way, you'll become more selective about your marriage partner. It's not all about lust, compatible tastes in furniture, and looking good in photographs together. Your spouse is your mirror. Keep this in mind when you don't like what you see.

Don't Rush Romance

I mourn the demise of patient, ardent seduction. Lovers just want to get into my girdle as quickly as possible these days. Slow down, I tell them. Take your time. A woman reaches her peak of flavor as she ages, like a fine cheese, just before becoming rancid and inedible. By stating this simple truth, you can make a suitor pause and think deeply.

The Heartbroken Shepherd

Once upon a time, in a region of France known for its many underground caves, a young man worked as a shepherd. Bored one day, he climbed into a cave. He began to eat his simple lunch of bread and sheep's milk cheese. Before he had swallowed the first bite, he heard the voice of a young woman singing outside. The shepherd scrambled to the cave entrance. It was love at first sight. He and the woman began a torrid affair that ended badly two months later when the woman ran off to Paris with the miller's daughter. Eventually, the shepherd found himself near the cave again. He looked for the lunch that he had left in the dank atmosphere. The cheese was furry with mold. To punish himself, the shepherd ate it anyway. Delicious. He was the discoverer of Roquefort cheese. Point being, sometimes heartache and self-loathing can help you overcome your natural disgust, allowing you to partake of something repulsive. But rarely will you find an undiscovered delicacy.

Look Up

A h, look to the clear night sky painted with stars. Starlight from ancient times has traveled mind-staggering distances to meet your gaze. Traditionally, human civilization has looked to the stars to plot a course forward and to find a way home. Now you have GPS devices to tell you where you are. Celestial navigation has become obsolete. You no longer get your bearings by looking at points of light far beyond your planet. Instead, you bounce a signal off a mirror held in your orbit. This is just one example of how nauseatingly self-referential you've become.

Look Out

Your situation reminds me of the first time I wore prescription eyeglasses to resolve my nearsightedness. I walked outside and was startled by so many bright stars in the sky, seemingly close enough to touch. They had been there all along, of course, but I was blind to them. Nowadays, with light pollution in most American cities, you see so few stars. You live in the glare of a spotlight. You can see what is close to you in clinical detail. Yet you are blind to the vast context in which you do your little dance.

FEBRUARY 20

Mixed Joys of Ownership

As you dream of acquiring gems, mansions, and sports cars, keep this in mind: It can be a grave misfortune to own something that others covet and would kill to own. Sure, that's a nice watch. It incites envy in many who see it. Why does this make you feel proud and important? You should feel like a crime statistic waiting to be tallied.

FEBRUARY 21

Hail to the Chief

When pressure became too much for Teddy Roosevelt, he would settle into a nice, warm bathtub in the dark and amuse himself for hours by holding a lit match over the water to ignite his flatus as it bubbled to the surface. Don't judge. The presidency is a stressful job.

FEBRUARY 22

Don't Be So Trusting

B e suspicious of things that come too easily. Nuts grow on trees, but you still have to crack them. Fish may jump into your boat, but you still have to gut them. Beware of hidden costs. Nothing worth having comes free, except the air you breathe. And legitimate questions can be raised about that, too.

FEBRUARY 23

What You Need

T he holier you claim you are, the more I think you're terrified of yourself. The more you denounce my life and values, the more clearly I see your fraudulence. The more you claim to have moral fiber, the more distinctly I hear you crying out for an enema.

When Dreams Are Foolish

Once upon a time, there was a young woman who dreamed of becoming a country music superstar. She wore cowboy shirts, a cowboy hat, white jeans, and white cowboy boots, even after Labor Day. She carried a guitar with her everywhere, to doctor appointments and on airplanes. She told me she was prepared at all times to be plucked from obscurity and made famous. She invited me to one of her shows at a coffeehouse in Tujunga. Her performance was embarrassingly bad. Afterward, she asked my opinion. I said it would be better, perhaps, if she practiced more. "I'm a natural," she laughed. "I don't need to practice." Dreams are foolish only if you fail to work hard to achieve them. A costume can take you only so far. And, if you carry a guitar, you'd better know how to play it. The woman eventually won fans as an online psychic healer, a career which suited her true talent for amplifying delusion.

Heed the Limits of Fantasy

Fantasy can be a psychological bridge to help you cross from trauma and turbulence to serenity and acceptance. For example, you may find yourself fantasizing about quitting your job, smiting your boss, defending yourself brilliantly in a dispute, or poisoning the rabbits in your garden. In each case, fantasy is a way of coping. You are too demoralized to quit your job, and you will never be articulate in the heat of an argument. Fantasizing helps you to absorb these hard facts. It is very likely, however, that you will poison the rabbits. For a moment, you will feel superior. Then you will feel worse than ever. Fantasy does not prepare you for how crappy you'll feel after fulfilling a perverse, self-indulgent fantasy.

Eating in Heaven and Hell

One vision of hell suggests that it's like sitting at a long banquet table filled with delicious food. Everyone at the table is forced to eat with unwieldy chopsticks that are too long. People go mad with frustration not being able to put food in their mouths. The vision of heaven is exactly the same. Except in heaven, people use their long chopsticks to feed the person across the table from them, so they all enjoy the banquet thanks to harmonious cooperation. Point being, if we simply help one another, we can transform hell into heaven. The analogy doesn't address what happens when people at one end of the table want more braised duck than they have, or when a cabal of diners monopolizes the *foie gras*. Heaven can turn ugly fast.

Your Search for Specialness

You can wander forever in search of something special. When you find something special, you hold it close. Soon it becomes ordinary to you. You set out again in search of something special. The trouble is your inability to see specialness in the ordinary, in that which is beyond any value or price. Consider the wonders of a robin's egg or my discarded coffee grounds. Some people are able to see Jesus in their waffles and popes in the grain of their wood-paneled rumpus rooms. If you can't, you're not really trying.

Fame Isn't a Musical

Fans are horrible. Do not wish for them. They inflate your ego out of proportion. Then, when you disappoint them—as you inevitably will—they snap and snarl like alley dogs. Fans feel that they have bestowed celebrity, therefore, it's theirs to rescind when the mood strikes. They don't love you. They don't want your happiness. They see you as their property. Celebrity is a curse. Avoid it if you can.

A Leap of Faith

When I refer to faith, I do not mean blind obedience or loony belief. I mean faith in the unseen, unproven, improbable, fundamental goodness of oneself and others. I mean faith that we and our fellows are motivated by more than self-interest and self-preservation. Such faith is risky, requiring a leap of optimism. Some people make this leap over and over, each time plummeting into a pit of disappointment. Optimism is one thing. Serial, reckless misjudgment is quite another. Look before you leap. Be discerning. It's a long way down.

A Note on Hexes

L et me get this straight. You wished ill upon your enemy. Nothing particularly ill befell your enemy, but your loved one ended up in the hospital. And you believe this misfortune is payback for your ill thoughts. Really? Then, by the same logic, believe thus: You wish good things for your enemy. Nothing particularly good befalls your enemy, but your loved one ends up happy and healthy as a result. Why are you wasting your time with hexes? You should be sending good thoughts to your enemies and reaping the benefits.

In Praise of Others

Y ou hate when others are praised, especially Bob, the VP of marketing. You've never liked him. You think he's a self-promoting slickster who dodges accountability. You cannot bear to see honors and accolades heaped upon him. But you would rejoice if he were pelted with insults and scorn. And it surprises you, genuinely, that he feels exactly the same way about you. Do yourself a favor. Sincerely wish for him to get a better job that he can lord over you for two weeks before he leaves your company—and your life—for good. The best way to get rid of someone is to wish him great success. Why can't you do this? Perhaps you don't want to get rid of him. Perhaps you need someone to despise so you'll never have to see how much you despise yourself. Heh.

Three Rules of Your Ex

1. Your Ex will never change. He will never be the person you want him to be.

2. You will never get what you want from Your Ex. Ultimately, you want him to not do what he did years ago. But what has been done cannot be undone.

3. Even if he paid twice as much in child support, it still would not be enough. No amount of compensation can bring back your wasted youth. So stop grasping for compensation. You will never receive it because of rules one and two.

Incompatible with Science

My critics have said that my teachings are incompatible with evolutionary biology, particularly my assertion that the universe is a conscious, living entity of capricious will that happens to despise evolutionary biologists. Am I being unscientific? Or are scientists being overly sensitive?

The Wise Owl

Once upon a time, there was a boy who lost three coins. Distressed, he searched for his missing money. He came upon a girl who was delighted because she had found three coins. The boy told her what he had lost. The girl's joy quickly faded as she handed her coins to the boy. Seeing how sad she was, the boy could feel no happiness. He said, "I cannot say for certain these coins belong to me. Let's ask the wise owl what to do." The boy and girl explained it all to the owl. The owl reached into his own pocket and produced a coin. He gave two coins to the boy and two coins to the girl. He said, "Today we each have lost a coin." The children were content. Never did they consider the peculiar, creepy implausibility of a talking owl with pocket change. Be alert.

Supplementary Rules of Your Ex

1. Your Ex is here to stay. Because of your children, plan on Your Ex being part of your life for the duration. Fantasizing about his sudden demise is mean-spirited and misdirected.

2. Your Ex is not your problem. Your problem now is how you deal with Your Ex. In trying to make your Ex pay and suffer, you have paid and suffered.

3. Your Ex is not the author of your life story, you are. You've made it the story of *How I Was Wronged*. If you want to fantasize about a sudden demise, imagine that all your hopes and expectations regarding Your Ex are dead, buried, and forever put to rest.

Heaven and Hell

An army soldier was about to be sent off to war. Concerned about his soul, he asked the army chaplain if he would go to hell if he were to kill someone in battle. The chaplain said, "A soldier like you is too stupid to understand anything about hell." At that, the soldier drew his gun on the chaplain, saying, "Damn you, chaplain." The chaplain nodded calmly. "Ah, my child, what you are feeling right now is the state of hell." Surprised, the soldier holstered his weapon and bowed, saying, "Thank you, teacher." Again, the chaplain nodded. "What you feel now is the presence of heaven. Heaven and hell exist nowhere but in our own hearts." The grateful soldier solemnly went back to his bunk and began packing his bag. But he never made it into battle because he was dishonorably discharged. Profound teaching or no, you don't pull a gun on a chaplain.

MARCH 8

Consolation

It's impossible to console you if you won't believe my comforting fictions," said the priest to the bereaved. "Sometimes being inconsolable is the only appropriate response to life," replied the bereaved. When you wish to console the inconsolable, a plate of sandwiches is more eloquent than religion.

MARCH 9

The Other Woman

It's not fair to blame The Other Woman for the infidelity of Your Ex. With whom did you have an agreement? Who broke the agreement? He might've misled her. He might've fibbed, saying that you two were separated, or that you had an open relationship. His deceptions were good enough to fool you, after all. Your rage toward The Other Woman is misplaced. Maybe she is a calculating piece of work, but that's no justification for keying her car.

MARCH 10

Making God Laugh

The wise have said, "If you want to make God laugh, tell him your plans." Another way is to anthropomorphize "him" and presume he has a sense of humor. Hilarious.

Catastrophe Looms

A h, we're hurtling toward doom. As a society. As a planet. It isn't because gay people want to get married and women want self-determination. It's because peaceful people turn their interests and energies toward leisure, amusement, and so-called convenience. Meantime, kingpins and cartels sharpen their knives.

A Quarrel

A divorcing couple argued about who should win custody of their dog, an adorable Yorkshire terrier named Winkle. One grabbed Winkle and ran outside. The argument continued on the sidewalk as neighbors, peering out windows, shook their heads at the familiar scene. The one holding Winkle walked into the street. Just then, a convertible was driving past. It's hard to say if Winkle leaped or was thrown into the passenger seat. Regardless, the dog was gone, long gone, as the convertible accelerated. The couple was stunned. Then they laughed and immediately halted divorce proceedings. They realized that people who use animals as pawns in cruel disputes deserve to live together in mutual torment. Quite so.

Science Versus Religion

I am content to let science reveal the laws of the physical world. I am content to let religion plumb the mysteries of human experience. I am fed up with those who demand that science and religion comply with the same standards and ultimately reach the same conclusions. That's like using the rules of basketball to evaluate whether one is good at math: unhelpful.

Meaning without God

Some of my friends claim that they don't believe in God. They do, however, believe in believing in God. Such a belief gives their lives meaning. I ask, "What exactly is the meaning, then?" My friends do not know, but they feel much better knowing that life means *something*. My darlings, this is existential laziness. On a related note, I am reminded of a song I used to love—a heartbreaking country-Western ballad about the death of a loyal dog. I loved it until I heard the songwriter explain that he had written it as a joke about his hated ex-wife. Never again could I appreciate that song. Knowing the creator's intent spoiled it for me, frankly. What does it matter what your life means to God? Far more relevant is what it means to you.

Ides of March

Julius Caesar was stabbed in the back by his trusted advisors on this very date, it is said. Supposedly, he was warned of the attack, yet the warning did not prevent the deed. Treachery takes on a wicked life of its own. It's tempting to believe that problems can be resolved and the world can be made better by bumping off the Dictator-in-Perpetuity using undemocratic methods. Such are the makings of tragedy. Beware the facile appeal of assassination, both literal and figurative. Beware saboteurs. When you're the boss, everyone wants to take you down.

Being a Good Person

If you have endured what you perceive to be injustice, you might develop the belief that you are owed something in exchange. You might be tempted to say, "I have suffered. Therefore, I am righteous and deserve to submit phony reimbursement requests." Similarly, if you have done something you consider praiseworthy—such as recycling your scotch bottles—you are likely to believe that it's okay to do something unkind. You mistakenly believe that suffering, sacrifice, and occasional good deeds make you a good person. Further, being a good person entitles you to behave shabbily on occasion. In truth, this way of thinking would never even occur to a good person.

Do Not Be Bullied by Your Whims

Your wants and whims have slapped you around for a long time. You think you are defined by your hunger. It must burn, or else you are lacking. It must be fulfilled, or else you have failed. Impulsive craving guides your life, leading you into shops, bars, and bedrooms. I have no quarrel with natural appetites; rather, compulsion is the bully. Stand up. Learn to say no to compulsion. It takes your lunch money and gives you a black eye.

The Month of War

The month of March is named for Mars, the Roman god of war. Mars isn't noble so much as he's strong, hardened by battle and almost giddy in his bloodlust. He just wants to wield weapons, blow stuff up, ruin villages, and revel in the carnage. He's very in-the-moment. He doesn't contemplate long-term effects or what comes after the destruction. His job is to slaughter, not to rebuild or restore. People nowadays seem to forget these fundamental qualities of Mars and the nature of war, as they're sipping cabernet at their local wine-and-small-plates establishment.

You Can't Help Yourself

I've never been more disappointed in anyone or anything. It's as if the childish, impulsive side of you is stronger than your will to live up to your promises. You apologize and say you want another chance. You're embarrassed by your bad behavior. You'll do better, you promise. But you don't. Your promises have no strength or seriousness behind them. Yes, of course, I forgive you. I forgive your lies and your faithlessness. But I can't forget that this is *how you are*. This is what you do. You lack discipline to take responsibility for yourself and to behave differently. You hate me for giving up on you, but you gave up on me a long time ago. I'm switching my mobile phone service, and there's nothing more to say.

Spring Perspective

With today's vernal equinox, we're in a new position relative to the sun. We were at a new and different angle yesterday, too. But today is special. The whole earth shifts its alignment and, accordingly, we expect a great shift in our lives. The only thing that has shifted is our perspective. This alone changes everything without really changing anything. Or does it?

A Note on the Equinox

If you're accustomed to living in the twentieth century, you probably assume that the vernal equinox falls on March 21. But this is no longer true. Please be aware that in the twenty-first century, the equinox falls on March 20. Nature is keeping us on our toes by switching it around. If ancient planets and calendars can change, certainly you can, too. My prescription for today: Move an item of furniture, if only imperceptibly. Shift the position of a chair. Turn a knickknack three degrees in a northerly direction. Something. Such changes are completely meaningless. Or are they?

Hero Worship

I request that you refrain from idolizing people you don't know personally. Do you know this person well enough to have heard him snore? Have you spent enough time with this person to have heard her tell the same witty anecdote over and over? If not, you do not know this person sufficiently to idolize him or her. In any case, what you're idolizing is not a person but a projection, an idea or ideal of a person based on conjecture, assumptions, skillful publicity and, mostly, your desire to idolize. It's a kind of willful blindness regarding reality. It bugs me.

Dilute the Poison

Poisons and pollutants surround us in varying concentrations. For example, a high concentration of colorless, odorless carbon monoxide in your home can kill you before you know you're dead. Yet the toxin is present in the atmosphere; when diluted with enough fresh air, it's not lethal. The same concept applies to your poisonous heart. I cannot hope to eradicate the poisons of greed, anger, and stupidity from your constitution. The best I can hope for is an enlargement of your capacity to be generous, patient, and wise. The poison is still there, but with a broader sense of purpose and improved ventilation, we all might survive.

Respect the Great Volcano Goddess

The great volcano goddess created an island with a lush, green, rainy side and a rocky, barren, dry side. A man from the dry side traveled to the rainy side. He exclaimed that the dry side was superior because there was more sunshine there. Without warning, the volcano goddess coughed up an enormous rock, which struck the man on the head, killing him instantly. Seeing this, people on the rainy side exclaimed that the rainy side must be superior because the volcano goddess favored it. In response, the volcano goddess belched a river of lava, fatally engulfing those who proclaimed the superiority of the rainy side. The volcano goddess created both sides of the island, after all. She could not bear to hear any of it disparaged by way of comparative evaluation. Remember this when tempted to boast about your homeland.

Better Living through Chemicals

Some people claim that their recreational use of drugs has made them better human beings. Consuming these substances has made them more relaxed, more open-minded, more insightful and keenly attuned to their surroundings. In fact, if it weren't for recreational drug use, they'd be self-involved no-funsters. Do not take their word for it. If you want to know whether drugs have made someone a better person, ask his or her coworkers, spouse, and children. You'll likely get a very different opinion.

Your Sense of Humor

Long ago on the island of Sardinia, those who were feeble and unable to contribute to society were fed a neurotoxic plant known as the "sardonic herb." The poison caused people to laugh bitterly and uncontrollably until they died. When I hear how mordant your laughter has become—and when I see how hard you laugh at the infliction of cruelty—I think you must have ingested this herb. Death throes contort you.

Don't Marry Out of Pity

Sometimes people don't know the difference between pity and love. Do you need to be needed? Do you think you can fix your lover's poor little broken wing? It's likely that you feel sorry for this person. Don't marry someone you pity. Over time, the feeling will curdle into unarticulated resentment that you both will express in bewildering ways. The more you try to prop him up, the more he'll rip you down. I'm still paying off the debt racked up by the last puppy I brought home from the pound.

Review Your Priorities

Are you concerned about what's on television more than what's in your drinking water? Do you know next to nothing about your city government and the policies of your mayor? Most people can't name the members of their city council, but they can recite the names of local football coaches and debate their competitive legacies in rich detail. People don't care where their food comes from as long as it's cheap and plentiful and there are snacks for the big game. Thomas Jefferson said that the price of liberty is eternal vigilance. What a quaint sentiment in a culture enslaved by apathy regarding the foundations of life and freedom. Sorry. That's a bit harsh of me to say. I get cranky when one of my favorite shows is cancelled.

Watch Your Voyeurism

Long ago, a huntsman hid in the woods and spied on the Greek Goddess Artemis as she bathed with her nymphs. To punish his voyeurism and to prevent the huntsman from bragging about what he had seen, Artemis turned him into a stag which was then eaten by the man's own hunting dogs. Perhaps you should take a lesson from the ancients and be careful where you point that camera-phone, Sonny. You presume that you're *entitled* to know who is frolicking with whom. You see sexuality as a public commodity rather than a private sacrament. Your prurient appetites are like rabid dogs that, frankly, *bite*.

Privacy Isn't Confining

The conventional wisdom is that if you're not out and loud about your sexuality, you're confined in a stuffy closet. The Greek Goddess Artemis suggests an alternative view. Her private world is the wide-open air, an expansive psychological freedom. Her eroticism is undomesticated—wild in the best sense—and deeply sacred. She represents harmony with the natural world and with our own nature. Even so, copulating on the park lawn during your lunch hour hardly seems appropriate. Get a room.

Taking It in Stride

Where I live, March is often the snowiest month of the year. The day after a blizzard, I was outside shoveling the snow from my sidewalk. I heard someone say, "Excuse me." I looked up to see a man standing in the road. He asked, "How long until I get to the nearest convenience store?" I looked at him sternly and said, "I can't tell you that." He said, "Thanks for nothing," and continued on his way. After he had walked several brisk paces, I called out, "You'll be there in twelve minutes." He wheeled around and shouted, "Why didn't you just say that in the first place?" I replied, "Because I had no idea how fast you were walking." So true. But he was too cold to appreciate my point.

April Fool's Day

In the long-ago days of the American Frontier, people valued raccoons for their warm, stylish pelts. Raccoons, resentful at not being valued for their inherent dignity, had nothing but contempt for the men who tried to trap them. If you know anything about raccoons, you know they love drinking whiskey and trying on high-heeled shoes. One day a group of raccoons found several jugs of whiskey in the forest. They sensed a trap. But, aside from the abandoned whiskey, there were no signs of human trappers. So they drank all the whiskey and continued on their way. Deeper into the forest, they found dozens of pairs of fabulous stilettos. The raccoons could not resist the chance to try them on and model them for one another. Sadly, within an hour of finding the shoes, all the raccoons were caught and skinned by clever fur traders. Nothing is easier to catch than a drunken raccoon in heels. Temptations are often traps. Let this be a lesson to you.

Right Place, Right Time

You must trust that you are always exactly where you need to be at exactly the right moment. Perhaps you are stuck in traffic on a freeway, low on gas, late for an appointment, hoping your bladder has room to expand just a little more. This is precisely where you need to be to see that this is not the life you want. You are in your cocoon of separateness going nowhere fast. How fitting.

Practical Jokes Are Tiresome

I have no patience for those who humiliate others with practical jokes. If you're going to humiliate someone, don't pretend there's something funny about it. Humiliation is a valuable service, and a serious one. Mind you, there is a difference between humiliation and degradation. The former is necessary to keep one's pride in check; the latter is an unnecessary assault on self-respect. If someone has placed confidence in you, it degrades both of you to fool him—for example, by switching the salt and the sugar when you know your friend takes sugar with his tea. Why must you undermine your friend with this act of veiled hostility and ruin a good cup of tea? What self-respecting person would want to be friends with you after that?

The Strict Training of Humiliation

Humiliation familiarizes one with the state of being humble, of feeling small. Perhaps we are proud of our knowledge, beauty, or status. Perhaps we walk around thinking we're better than others. An episode of humiliation—such as a scolding from a beloved aunt—can help to wipe away arrogance, which is a dreadful poison. People who have never felt what it's like to be humbled tend to fear it. They puff themselves up bigger and bigger. They argue and resist humiliation by degrading others. Such people are outwardly boastful and insulting, but inwardly they are afraid of feeling small. Perhaps I should speak only for myself.

Control Your Guns

There's no such thing as an unloaded gun. Regard all firearms as deadly. Do not wave your barrel carelessly in my direction and say, "Don't worry. It's not loaded." Funny. Mine is loaded, and my inclination is to defend myself with force. Lucky for you, I can't hit the broad side of your buttocks even when I'm wearing my eyeglasses. Most certainly we are both safer with our guns than without them.

Training Is a Must

If you plan to own a gun, I insist that you avail yourself of formal, certified safety training. When I tell this to women, they usually agree wholeheartedly. But men often assume that a gun is self-explanatory and an extension of male anatomy, if you will. They can make it go "bang," and that's all they care to know. Ah, there's much to learn about a smooth draw, hitting a target and developing the discipline to whip it out only when lawful and appropriate.

Do Not Cherish High-Sounding Opinions

Half the time, people are full of crap. Well-intentioned crap is still crap. Live your own life. Find out for yourself what's what.

What Are You Practicing?

If you want to learn to play a sport or musical instrument, or become good at anything at all, you must practice. We all practice something repetitively, whether we're conscious of it or not. Perhaps we practice belittling others, selling ourselves short, or blocking our intuitive awareness. You would gladly tell your friends that you practice yoga or judo, but you probably wouldn't announce that you're practicing arrogance, self-sabotage, or alienation of affection. What are you practicing in secret?

Reality Cannot Be Trained

If we repeat something enough, it becomes second nature. This is how we train ourselves. Some people believe that we can train our thought patterns this way, too. For example, by repeating "prosperous" slogans, some people believe they can train themselves to attract wealth and abundance. They seem to forget, however, that reality is not a person and cannot be trained. Certainly, you can beseech the sky to rain money on you, and you can enact a series of rituals that you believe will coax gold coins from the clouds. But this kind of hoodoo doesn't even work on slot machines. Believe me, I've tried.

APRIL 10

About the Help

If you're hiring a nanny, personal assistant, groundskeeper, or tennis instructor, choose someone toward whom you feel no romantic impulses, and vice versa. This is probably contrary to the principles of equal-opportunity employment and human nature. But trust me. The best way to fight temptation is to not have it around all the time dependent on you for a paycheck.

APRIL 11

Aside to a Philanderer

You claim you were seeking freedom. Well. When you're not honest with others, you deprive them of freedom. When you deny or withhold crucial facts from people, you're taking away their freedom to make informed choices. Freedom? Hah. "Escape" is more like it. Next time, just go to the movies.

Jungles Will Be Jungles

During the heyday of the Khmer empire, a king built a grand Buddhist monastery in the midst of a Cambodian jungle. No expense was spared to construct the immense, elaborate temple of intricately carved stone. It was built to endure forever. But, as decades passed, riches were exhausted. Populations relocated. The temple was forgotten for hundreds of years. Eventually, it was rediscovered—eerie, crumbling, entwined by serpentine roots of trees. The jungle was reclaiming it. The jungle takes hold of even our most lofty ambitions and turns them back into the earth from which they arose. Today's landmark public works project is tomorrow's Ta Prohm.

You Will Fall Down

When you fall, you push yourself up from the ground. You can't defy gravity completely, but you can work with it. Every time you fall, you push yourself back up, and you grow a bit stronger, or weaker, depending. It becomes a kind of friendly game. Gravity will win in the end; it will hold and keep you. But you continue to play the game because that's how the game is played: by continuing to get up.

Priestly Generosity

Late one night, a priest awoke to find a thief robbing the church office. The priest confronted the thief and asked, "My son, why are you robbing the house of the Lord?" The thief sobbed, "Because I am poor and hungry." The priest gave the thief a laptop computer, several ledger books, and money from a safe, and sent the thief on his way, promising he would not call the police until the man was long gone. The thief, humbled and grateful, ran away and never robbed anyone again. The priest went outside and admired the full moon, saying: "Poor fellow. I wish I could give him this beautiful moon. More than he will ever know, he has helped to conceal my embezzlement."

A Taxing Day

Let us all be silent for a moment and reflect upon our ambivalent feelings toward income tax. If we are paying it, it is because we earned some income. Hooray. Now let us reflect upon the roads, bridges, uplifting institutions, waste, and fraud supported by our hard-won pay—and the wars. Let's not forget the wars. It's a privilege to contribute taxes to live in a free, democratic nation. It's also a bitter price to pay. Poor indeed are the rich who won't part with pennies; poorer still are those whose taxes subsidize the rich.

Rinse, Rinse, Rinse

My wise words are so pithy that you probably want to memorize them and repeat them often. Please don't. I want to wash you clean. My words are like sudsy soap. If you fail to rinse away my words after they have done their work, you will be coated with waxy film. You will not be clean. I am brainwashing you in the best sense of the word. True brainwashing leaves no traces.

Nasal Lavage

While you're rinsing your brain, consider rinsing your nose. At most drug stores, you can purchase a plastic syringe or bottle that shoots several ounces of saline into your sinuses, loosening mucus that may harbor microbial unpleasantness. A more gentle and traditional approach is to use a neti pot to pour salty solution in one nostril and out the other. This creates a vacuum effect that draws mucus out of the sinuses. The practice was developed by the yogis of ancient India to wash away ailments of the eyes, ears, and upper respiratory system. In addition, it promotes clarity of thinking and meditative insight. Of course, the ancient yogis had to make these claims. Otherwise, people would have no interest in pouring water up their noses. It stings.

Metaphoric Blindness

One dark night, a wise man gave a flashlight to a blind man. "A light is of no use to me," the blind man shrugged. The wise man insisted he take the light with him on the dark path, explaining, "Others will be able to see your light and make way for you." The blind man took the flashlight and went running down the path as he always did on his way home. He hadn't run a hundred yards before he collided with a farmer and knocked them both to the ground. Angry, the blind man said, "Didn't you see my flashlight?" The farmer picked up the light, toggled the switch, and said, "You need to turn it on first." The blind man, frustrated by the uselessness and complication of the flashlight, told the farmer to give it back to the wise man. Later that night, he ran recklessly into an oncoming ox cart and died on the spot. Point being, the metaphorically blind do not value metaphoric illumination, and the story ends badly.

Regarding Reputation

One day I was briefly trapped in an elevator with a reviled television commentator. This person had a reputation for shrill humorlessness, but I found her engaging and kind. I asked her, "Why do people hate you?" Wistful, she said, "When the sun shines brightly, sunbathers will be happy, but others will curse the heat and glare. When it rains, people with thirsty lawns will rejoice, but party planners hosting outdoor events will curse the downpour. People who find fault with the sun and rain can find fault with anything, even me." I nodded at these sage words, understanding instantly why she was so despised. She likens herself to forces of nature. I can see how that would rankle.

Projecting

When you're in love, it's as if the birds all sing to you, the flowers all smile, and trees nod hello. The same is true when you are high on hallucinogens. Why must you attribute human emotions and motives to everything, including plants and birds? Why is everything about you? You don't take it personally when birds crap on your car, do you? Ah, maybe you should.

A Note on Saving and Recycling

Once upon an airline flight, I was seated in first class next to a man who is internationally famous. I will not name him because I do not wish to embarrass him. When this gentleman was served scotch and a little packet of snacks, he took his chewing gum from his mouth and stuck it to his glass. He ate his snacks and drank his scotch with the wad perched on the rim. Later, he put the gum back in his mouth. Money cannot buy class, but it can obtain a fresh stick of gum. If you must remove gum from your mouth for any reason, wrap it in a bit of paper and dispose of it in the trash. Under no circumstances is chewed gum to be displayed, reused, or recycled.

Earth Day

Fresh air. Sunshine. Clean water. We live in paradise. The earth is like our loving mother who gives us life and everything that we need to sustain ourselves. Planet Earth is the Big Roxy Macallan from which we have emerged like babies. How disgusting, then, that we spew carbons on our own mother. It is a shame that you do not treat our Planet Earth with the same consideration that you show your mother. Actually, it's not surprising, considering how shabbily women are treated in general. Imagine if "respecting women" were a social trend or marketing fad on par with "going green," and everyone were harangued into regarding the exploitation of women as antithetical to human health and survival. My, how subversive I have become in my old age.

APRIL 23

Find a New Way

It is time for you to rethink who you are. You are no longer defined by your ability to cajole and coerce, buy and sell, whine and complain, strut and swagger. Find a new way. It's time to stop dressing like a teenager.

APRIL 24

Champing at the Bit

You have postponed and dillydallied long enough, you feel. You are eager to push ahead and make things happen. But wait. Are you pushing ahead because you see clearly what you need to do? Or because you hate to stand back and wait for an opening to present itself? I'm not suggesting that perhaps you're being petulant and pigheaded right now, but it wouldn't be the first time.

Oddities of Easter Observance

In some lands, spring festivals of renewal and joy are celebrated by administering ceremonial whippings with pussy willow switches. In some lands, children paint eggs and many people eat ham. In others, a bonfire is lit to symbolize the return of radiance. I mark the day by practicing the hula. It's in the wrists and hands as much as the hips. Whatever rekindles passion for life is a worthy observance. Go easy on the sacramental wine, monsignor.

To Be Wise

To be wise, first you must understand what it is to be foolish. A foolish person believes that he or she is reasonable, rational, or wise. By contrast, a wise person never underestimates his or her capacity for foolishness. When we behave foolishly, rarely do we recognize it until after the fact, if then. We believe so firmly in our rightness that we can't even imagine we're wrong. This is a warning sign of foolishness. But, being foolish, we interpret it as confirmation of our wisdom. True wisdom comes from long experience of being victimized by one's own foolishness. It's like knowing when you're about to faint and having the presence of mind to sit down and breathe.

Comparative Suffering

In this life, everyone suffers excruciating agony. How can this be true, you ask, when so many people live in relative ease and comfort while others starve? Ah, I do not claim that suffering is equitable. One size does not fit all. Still, comparing your suffering to that of others is pointless. The specifics vary, but the generality of suffering is universal; we all are subject to the pain of ceaseless change, illness, and loss. No one gets out alive. It's what you do with your suffering that's interesting. Does it crush you? Or does it polish you to glittering gem-like perfection? Hint: It crushes you. It crushes everyone.

Flossing Is Not Always Laudable

We had just eaten a delicious lunch in an upscale restaurant. A member of our party pulled out a length of dental floss and started to floss her teeth right there at the table. We all pretended not to notice. I was too appalled to say anything, a crime of silence for which I will never forgive myself. I helped to perpetuate this woman's mistaken assumption that dental hygiene is appropriate in public. Now I tell everyone: Floss at the table, and I will garrote you with that minty thread.

The Overflowing Tea Cup

A bright young man came to visit me one day. I invited him into my parlor for tea. He was the most extraordinary physical specimen, tall and strong, with classical features, resembling Michelangelo's *David*. At the tea table, he explained that he wanted to learn how to levitate. He asked that I become his teacher. I was pouring his tea as he spoke. I overfilled his cup, and a pool of tea flooded the table. He nodded with gratitude. "Yes, I see," he said. "You cannot fill a cup that is already full. I will empty my mind and let you fill me with your wisdom." Actually, I was merely distracted by his handsomeness. But it's a good lesson.

Happy in Excrement

Have you noticed that flies and worms are attracted to excrement? They love it. To them, being in excrement is like gorging on an all-you-can-eat buffet in a luxury hotel. But to us it's foul, stinky excrement. We'd never want to live in it, eat it, or hatch our young within its folds. So think about this: What if many things we regard as delightful, luxurious, or delicious are, from the perspective of higher intelligence, the equivalent of eating excrement? It puts chocolate éclairs in a potentially unflattering light.

May Day

The first day of May is often associated with socialism, labor-union activism, and the distress signal, "mayday." For me, it means none of these things. Rather, I recall a simpler time when, in courtship, young people would make May baskets filled with sweets and flowers and hang them anonymously on the doorknob of a would-be sweetheart. The trick was to ring the bell and run away. The receiver was meant to chase after the giver to win a kiss. Many genteel customs of the past were invented as excuses for kissing. That's when kissing was something one yearned for and looked forward to over many dreary months of kisslessness. Times are different now, with everyone slobbering over one another like Labradors at a dog park.

Like the Jacaranda

Many people are like the Jacaranda tree. Their lavender blossoms float like purple clouds above the streets of cities like Los Angeles and Brisbane. Everyone delights in the magical splendor. Everyone, that is, except for people whose parked cars are littered with fallen, rotting Jacaranda blossoms. They curse the damnable trees. Like the Jacaranda: Pretty at a distance, but you wouldn't want it all over your windshield.

Covetousness Can Kill You

In an Irish coastal town of yore, people relied on fish from the sea for their food and economic prosperity. Men spent all day fishing to provide for their families. One man was rather a bully. Each day he would row his boat around to the others, demanding a share of each man's catch. The bully would beat them severely if they did not comply. "Be grateful I don't take it all," he would sneer. Finally, the fishermen agreed on a plan. At the end of the day, each fisherman emptied his entire catch into the bully's boat. Soon, his boat was filled with fish. Yet more fishermen kept coming, dumping their fish, and then rowing away toward shore. Before long, the bully's boat sank under the weight, and he drowned. No one was sad. Be grateful that you do not receive everything you covet, especially if you are a lazy boor.

Don't Be Suckered by the Robe

People who wear ceremonial robes—academics, judges and priests—are revered mostly for what their costume conveys: They have studied sacred texts, and they know things that we cannot know. They are elevated and protected from scrutiny by a shroud of authority. Under their robes they're just as naked and ungainly as the rest of us. No, it's not something I want to see. But it's a perspective to keep in mind when your appeal is denied, for example. No one is infallible.

Someone Is Always Watching

Some of my friends are happy to know that God is always watching. They believe that God operates a kind of cosmic security-monitoring system that records all thoughts, words, and deeds for future judgment. Many of these friends similarly feel that it's appropriate for the government to keep ordinary citizens under constant surveillance. "If you're not doing anything wrong, why object to being monitored?" they ask. First, I object to the implication that a police state is a reflection of God—and that God is a *police* God. But mostly I find it oppressive and unsettling when my cat stares at me, let alone the unblinking eye of omnipresent bureaucracy.

MAY 6

Like Lilacs

Many people are like my lilac bushes. Lilacs require a cold winter. Their roots must be gripped by hard-frozen ground. Otherwise, they won't produce their luxurious, fragrant blooms in spring. To blossom, sometimes it is necessary to be chilled to the core.

MAY 7

Prayers of Desperation

Prayers of desperation are the best prayers. When we are in a state of reckless despair, dogma and calculation go out the window. Formulas and plans are abandoned. No longer cautious or hopeful, we pray boldly for the impossible. It takes great courage and great pain to birth a marvel, or to even try.

Parable of The Skilled Physician

Long ago, there was a skilled physician who had many obnoxious sons. The doctor developed a potion that would cure the young men of their swagger and sense of entitlement. Two sons drank it and became bearable, but the rest refused, insisting that there was nothing wrong with them. Disappointed, the physician hatched a plan. He traveled far away and sent a messenger to tell his sons that he had died in a foreign land. When his sons received the news, they were devastated. As they were preparing for their father's memorial service, they remembered the potion he had made for them. In their grief, they drank the potion and instantly became kind, patient, caring people. The messenger reported to the father that the plan had worked. The father returned home, and the whole family rejoiced. If his sons hadn't taken the medicine and become kind, they probably would have killed the skilled physician because, honestly, that was a pretty messed up stunt.

The Cult of Skepticism

I am suspicious of people who provide personal, emotional testimony about the wonders of a new belief system, product, or affinity group. These testimonials follow a familiar pattern: "I was deeply troubled in some way, but then I adopted this belief system, started using this product or joined this group—now I'm happy and fulfilled." We are all suckers for this pitch. When you hear it, consider the possibility that you're being hoodwinked. I was once a sucker, but then I became a skeptic. Now I'm happy and fulfilled.

Spiritual Prescriptions

Spiritual guidance is as powerful as any drug. It's not to be handed out willy-nilly. You need to see a medical doctor to get a prescription for medicine, yet you gobble up guidance that's given out indiscriminately like pills at a rock concert. No wonder you're confused.

MAY 11

Dangerous Indulgence

Great sages have said that the wanton pursuit of fleeting pleasures—such as sex, fame, and intoxication—is like a toddler licking butter-cream frosting off a razor blade. To any sane onlooker, this is a perilous, horrifying situation that demands intervention. But in our degenerate state, most of us just think, "Mmm. Frosting."

MAY 12

Cheer Up

I must chide you for your self-hatred. Perhaps secretly you feel insignificant, as if everyone except you is living a wonderful life. You suspect that everyone despises you, or everyone regards you with cold indifference. I find it astonishing that you can even think such a thing. Truth is, most people don't even know you and couldn't care less. Cheer up.

Half a Steak

There once was a young man who loved to eat steak. Whenever he would buy a steak, he would cut it in two and fry the pieces separately. "Why do you do that?" his roommate asked. "Because that's the way we have always cooked steak in my family." His mother and her mother cooked steak the same way. Later, the man visited his great-grandmother, who was on her deathbed. He asked, "Great-grandmother, why do we always cut steak in half before we fry it?" She said: "Because I didn't have a pan large enough to fit a whole steak." Some customs are mere multigenerational misunderstandings.

Trying to Be Pure

Trying to be perfect, pure, or pristine is like eating an ice-cream cone in a sandstorm. You can't have ice cream without getting a mouthful of grit, too. Forget the ice cream. Just accept your fundamental foulness, and get on with doing your best.

The Foul and the Fabulous

Look at it this way. You are like a nugget of gold wrapped in a slice of rancid bacon. You are like a diamond wedged in a putrid cut of sirloin steak. You are a mass of rotting meat, yet you contain something priceless that cannot be corrupted by the flesh that surrounds it. The gold cannot exist outside the bacon; the diamond cannot be separated from the steak. Do you see? The foul and the fabulous coexist simultaneously in every moment of your life.

Kitchen Fairy

A woman went to her local mystic and explained that an angel came each afternoon to her kitchen. She wanted to know the meaning of this. "What does it look like?" the mystic asked. "It looks like a sparkling light on the wall," the woman said. "It comes every day at the same time." The mystic thought for a moment. "Heaven doesn't diddle around. Seeing a real angel should freak you out and alter the course of your life. Maybe what you're seeing is sun reflected off polished chrome." The woman said no more. She went home convinced the mystic was a phony. Most people prefer to cling to small, harmless illusions rather than see something life-changing. You say you want to see the face of heaven, but do you really?

Protector Goddess Cow

The ruler of an ancient Chinese kingdom wrongly banished two faithful servants because of a convoluted dispute. Far on the outskirts of the kingdom, the servants foraged for food but were slowly starving. Because they had been falsely convicted, heaven took pity on them and sent them a protector goddess in the form of a lovely, fat dairy cow. The servants were thrilled. They had never tasted such delicious milk. At last, they were full and happy. Soon, however, they grew complacent. One said to the other, "The cow's milk is so delicious, just think how delicious her meat must be. Let's eat her." Hearing this, the cow ran away, leaving the servants to starve. How quickly gratitude gives way to greedy thoughts and greedy words. Such a shame.

MAY 18

Postcard from Hell

The road to hell is paved with celebrity gossip. When you get to hell, you'll notice everyone is super skinny because they can't eat. If they ever manage to eat, they instantly barf. Everyone in hell thinks everyone else looks more fabulous than they do. Plastic surgery is unlimited, free and endless, because everyone is competing to look better than everyone else. Hell is a mass-delusional eating-disordered land. Inhabitants think they're in heaven, but nonresident visitors are frightened by the ghoulishly distorted bodies and faces that they see. Or maybe I'm thinking of Los Angeles.

MAY 19

Swapping Gossip

Friendship based on swapping gossip is not to be trusted. Any person who gossips with you will gossip about you. Good gossips will prod you to share a confidence or two and will swear strictest secrecy. But your dish will be on the street faster than a stolen passport. Don't traffic in dirt if you don't want to get buried.

MAY 20

Nobility in Loss

In a hard-fought contest there's as much nobility in losing as in winning. To put up a spirited fight is its own glory. There's no nobility in winning or losing, however, if you are ungracious. Take your showboating and sulking off the field of play. The sport is bigger than you—bigger, even, than your conception of yourself.

Foolish Compassion

One day a poor vagrant appeared at the door of a remote temple and asked for food. The junior monk, excited at the opportunity to show off his compassion, invited the vagrant inside for dinner. The junior monk brought him to the table. The chief monk looked hard at the vagrant and said, "This man is obviously a dangerous criminal. He is welcome to eat with us, but I insist that he leave after the meal." The junior monk assumed that the strength of his compassion was being tested. After they had eaten, he pleaded with the chief monk to let the vagrant spend the night in the temple. The chief monk relented, saying, "Fine. If you are willing to accept responsibility for the consequences, he may stay." During the night, the vagrant hacked the chief monk to bits with an ax, looted the temple, and ran away. In the morning, gazing at the gruesome remains of his teacher, the junior monk realized that the abstract ideal of compassion should never be allowed to trump a gut feeling of danger.

A Sign

Trying to find your divinity is like looking for your misplaced car keys. The more dramatic and frantic your search, the farther you move from what you seek. Just relax. It's right where you left it. It will come to you. If not, there's nothing wrong with public transportation. Maybe it's a sign from the great Roxy Macallan that you should forsake your car and find a new way of living. As soon as you convince yourself that you don't need those keys, they'll turn up somehow.

MAY 23

What's That Smell?

It is time to consider the possibility that you are full of yourself. You have postponed serious consideration of this point long enough. You do not want to think that you are in any way conceited or arrogant. No. You are noble and righteous yet misunderstood. Everyone else is misguided. Ah, yes. You have grown so fond of your own stink that you no longer smell it.

MAY 24

Good Intentions

Actions taken because of good intentions do not always have good results. When you try to help people, you usually become a nuisance. Why must you hover around the kitchen when I'm trying to put dinner on the table?

Gift Card in the Sport Coat

Two men who had been great friends in high school had not seen each other in years. One was rich while the other was poor. The rich man invited the poor man to his home for dinner. As they drank their third bottle of wine and talked about old times, the poor man remarked, "All I have is this Harris tweed sport coat." Soon, he passed out drunk and the rich man, taking pity on his friend, slipped into a pocket of his coat a golden, prepaid credit card representing a lavish sum. Months later, the poor man called his friend from jail. The rich man bailed him out and listened to his tale of woe. Since the night they'd had dinner, the poor man's life had gotten worse; he was homeless and ill. "But you still have your coat," the rich man observed, and he directed the other to reach into a pocket for the credit card. "I can't believe you didn't find it. You see, all along you have possessed the means of freeing yourself from your dreadful circumstances." The poor man replied, "I wish you would have mentioned it sooner." What good is wealth if you don't know you have it?

People Are Impossible

Have you noticed how people look down on the poor? They shun them. They criticize them for being the architects of their own poverty. Have you noticed how people despise the rich? They flatter them to their faces, but when their backs are turned, they criticize the rich for not being worthy of their own wealth. People are impossible.

People Are Intolerable

Have you noticed how people are envious of those they regard as their superiors, resenting them bitterly? And yet, these same people put on airs and lord their status over those they think are beneath them. If they regard someone as an equal, they will bicker with him and complain about him to gain the upper hand. People are intolerable.

Stay Away from Childish People

Childish people will waste your life. Be courteous, but keep them at arm's length. Childish people are the ones who must have their own way. They alone are to be praised; others are to be criticized. They alone deserve attention; others are to be ignored. They alone are righteous and accomplished; others amount to nothing. It is better to be alone than to be in the company of childish people.

Focus on What's Important

Decades ago in a rural penitentiary, a prisoner was being led to his execution. The warden told the prisoner that his life would be spared if only he could do one thing. He handed the prisoner a brimming mug of coffee. "I want you to walk down the road to the gate and back without spilling a drop." The prisoner went on his way. The guards said to the warden, "That's so easy. Why are you letting him do that?" The warden laughed. "Along the road are buxom women, several kinds of liquor, and an accordionist. Surely, the prisoner will be distracted and spill the coffee." Eventually, the prisoner returned. The cup was still full to the brim. The prisoner's life was spared. The warden asked: "What did you think of the ladies, booze, and entertainment out there, prisoner?" The prisoner responded, "What are you talking about? The only thing I saw was this cup of coffee." Meaning, when you regard your task as a matter of life and death, you don't even notice distracting temptations. Focus.

MAY 30

Memorial Day

Today we are asked to recall those who served as soldiers and gave up their lives in war. Initiated by freed slaves after the Civil War, this day was set aside to honor fallen Union soldiers and to strew their graves with spring flowers. Later, the remembrance was extended to Confederate soldiers, too. Since then, there have been so many wars, and so many dead—so much barbarism and futility. It is a day to honor the victors while knowing there are no victors, and to mourn the loss.

MAY 31

Winning by Losing

You lack character. This is the greatest calamity of our time. The best thing you can do to help humankind is to undertake a project with all your heart and soul. Then fail miserably, making no excuses. This would build character. Humankind is counting on you to fail. Don't let us down.

A Month of Roses

I'm so glad it's finally June. Now we can talk about something important: Weddings. June is the month of matrimony, named for the goddess Juno, queen of brides. In mythology, Juno was married to Jupiter. She was also Jupiter's sister, but don't let that nettlesome detail taint the blissful veil through which you ought to view the month of June. This is a month of roses, not thorns. Or so we all would like to believe. Believe a little harder, now. This is the merry month of make-believe. No marriage can survive without it.

Think Positively

Positive thinking is a powerful technique. By repeating mantras of success and happiness, your brain will start to think positively. Your body, in turn, will function positively. Your life will become a thundering triumph of positive reinforcement. The crux of positive thinking is a wonderful phenomenon known as self-hypnosis. By convincing yourself of your success and happiness, you don't necessarily become happier and more successful. You do, however, reframe the events of your life to fit the story you're telling yourself— that you're happier and more successful. You're not altering reality; you're altering your perception of reality. In this regard, positive thinking is far superior to drugs and alcohol. It's a chemical-free, no-calorie trip to nowhere.

Airboy

A young boy awoke one morning to find an airplane outside his home. The boy put on his robe and went to investigate. The craft was small, like a bathtub with wings. He saw no engine or propeller. There were no controls. "A toy," he thought, as he climbed in. The plane took off and soared over his house. At first he was afraid, but then he thought, "Grandma." The plane flew to his grandmother's house and landed in her yard. The boy knocked, but no one was home. "She's at work," the boy thought as he returned to the plane. Then he remembered: "School." Within minutes, he landed on the school playground. His friends came running to admire the plane. They asked, "Where did it come from? How does it fly?" The boy said, "I don't know.

Come fly with me." But his friends declined. They were afraid. "I'll fly with you," said the boy's younger sister. The two flew to see the pyramids of Giza and returned home for lunch before anyone knew they were missing, which seems like a tragedy of neglect. But when you can fly just by imagining, and you have someone who believes in you, everything will work out okay

"Protective eyewear is a mark of good sense."

Affirm Your Confirmation Bias

What's wrong with self-hypnosis? If repeating a mantra makes you feel happier and more successful, what's wrong with that? If you learn nothing else, learn one thing: you tend to notice only what supports your own beliefs and opinions, and you block out everything else. Smarty-pants sociologists call this "confirmation bias." This is what makes you human. You think you know what's what, but you're seeing only part of the story. You systematically misperceive the world. You just do. Positive thinking is confirmation bias on steroids. It's willful, self-imposed blindness that you mistake for a cure-all.

Fast and Slow Oxen

Once upon a time, two farmers drove their ox carts toward the town market. One cart was pulled by a fast ox, and it drove far ahead. The farmer driving the slow cart yelled at his ox, "You're too slow. What's wrong with you? Stupid ox." As the farmer cursed and chastised, the ox walked slower and slower. When he finally reached the market, he approached the other farmer. "How much do you want for your fast ox?" The man traded his fast ox for the slow one, plus a tidy sum of money. The next week, on the same road, the farmer with the supposedly slow ox passed the farmer with the supposedly fast ox. The farmer cursed the animal: "You were fast last week. What is wrong with you? Lazy, no-good ox." When he arrived at the market, he yelled at the other farmer: "You tricked me. My old ox is fast, and this one is slow." The other farmer explained. "It's no trick. I praise the ox. Without it, I would not be able to support my family. I thank the ox. That is why the oxen are eager to help me." The other farmer felt like an idiot, as well he should.

Everyone Needs a Little Encouragement

Give yourself a pep talk in the morning. Be grateful for who you are and what you have. Thank your body—kidneys, lungs, bowels, fat, and bones. Do some stretching if you can. Thank your senses—thank your eyes, ears, nose, mouth, and skin for providing a way for you to experience the world. Take a minute to appreciate your hair, wherever it may grow, whether sparse or abundant. Hair. Wow. What a mystery. This is not an exercise in evaluating yourself in relation to arbitrary beauty standards. This is no time to find fault. Your body is your ox. It will haul you through the day. You can't trade it for another. Give it some encouragement.

Be Discerning

When did children's candy become ironic? Banana-flavored taffy is marketed as "earwax." Jelly beans are available in flavors such as "dirt" and "snot." Gummy worms are popular. Candy has to be disgusting or extremely sour to capture a child's interest nowadays. In my day, a child was happy with a peppermint stick or licorice whip. Granted, we had to work ten-hour shifts in a textile mill to afford our sweets. But we knew the difference between candy and crap.

Find Solace in Simplicity

When I was a child, a favorite candy was a small paraffin bottle filled with sugar syrup. I would chew the chunk of wax for hours to get all the sweetness out of it. Then I would wrap the wax around a piece of string to make a candle. This is how I accidentally set the hay wagon ablaze, which was not as bad as the time I nearly choked on a lump of wax. Today when you offer wax to a child, he's likely to look quizzically at you. The young have no appreciation.

The Goddess and the Marriage Proposal

Once upon a time in Las Vegas, a man fell in love at first sight and asked a woman to marry him. Little did he know, she was a celestial goddess who planned to teach him a lesson for making a rash proposal. They went to a wedding chapel. The goddess gazed into the groom's starry eyes and asked, "Will you love me forever?" "Yes, always," the groom replied. "Even if I were a man?" The goddess transformed herself into a man. The groom was shocked. "I can't marry you now. Marriage is between a man and a woman." So the goddess transformed the groom into a woman. "Now we can be married." The groom was horrified. "This is all wrong. I want to marry the woman I proposed to." The goddess resumed her female form. "So it's a lesbian wedding." "No," the groom shouted. "I'm a man. I want a wife." The goddess changed him back into a man. "I can't marry you," she said. "You're already married to narrow understanding of gender." Another bad night in Vegas.

Beware of Instant Intimacy

Is it love at first sight? Fine. Give it some time to ferment and bubble before you sign away your rights, assets, or credit rating to another person. Trust and intimacy take time to develop. Three weeks or months of bonding can feel like an eternal love connection. But what's the rush? Some people cannot bear to be alone. At the same time, they cannot bear to be quiet and settled in a relationship for long. They careen from one affair to another, seeking intensity. They foolishly believe that intensity is passionate love. They will make promises aplenty in the heat of their adventure. But intensity will fade and promises will be forgotten. Beware of instant lovers. They're constantly fleeing from themselves.

King Kamehameha Day

Today we honor a monarch, Hawaiian King Kamehameha, who was brutal in his war to unite the islands. One day the king chased a fisherman across a rocky coast. The king's foot slipped and became wedged in the rocks. Seeing that the king was trapped, the fisherman told him, "I'm a non-combatant. I want no part of your war. Please stop trying to kill me." With that, he hit the king over the head with a canoe paddle and ran away. The incident apparently made quite an impression. Kamehameha later proclaimed that harming civilians during war was strictly off-limits. This was called the "Law of the Splintered Paddle." True story. Sometimes you have to hit leaders over the head to convince them to do the right thing.

JUNE 12

It Matters

The universe is like an ongoing soap opera. There's no limit to the chaos, dissolution, rebirth, and reformation that our universe goes through, again and again, over billions and trillions of centuries. Our life span, relative to everything else, amounts to little more than a snap of the fingers. You are as tiny and brief as a firefly, but you're not inconsequential. You do not comprehend the vastness of time and space, but that does not mean you can goof off.

JUNE 13

Chew Your Food

Your mouth is an important part of your digestive system. The way you eat, I would never guess. You eat as if the goal is to get food into your stomach as quickly as possible. This is all wrong. I insist that you chew your food thoroughly before you swallow it. Use your teeth. Work up some saliva. Chew until the food in your mouth has become a flavorless paste. Then—and only then—you may swallow. You overeat and become bloated yet malnourished because you refuse to take the time to chew. You should spend a good half hour eating a modest sandwich.

Dealing with Loneliness

With everyone around you getting married this month, you may find that your feelings of loneliness are accentuated, especially if you yourself are married. No matter how many people surround you, you will feel lonely if you think that "relationships" are arrangements you agree to conduct with others, something like contracts with rules and responsibilities. If, however, you understand that the whole of life is relationship, you'll find you're never lonely. You are in relationship with everything and everyone around you. You are in relationship with all human history, and all things yet to come. Your feelings of separateness and isolation are a bad dream—or, possibly, a defense mechanism if you're surrounded by losers.

Making Progress?

At the beginning, you felt as if you were making progress. You felt good. But now you are less enamored of your grand spiritual undertaking. It's not as fun as you had hoped. Instead you would like to do something to reinforce your sense of self-importance. You've come to the wrong place. There's no such thing as progress. Rather, we only perfect our powers of self-deception.

What Happened to Our Unassuming Folksiness?

The worst thing that ever happened to America is that we became enamored of pretention. We became a nation of braggarts and blowhards. We have survived surprise attacks, economic depression, civil war, and disputed elections. But our vainglory, affectation, and imperiousness may prove to be our undoing, along with drinking too much soda.

JUNE 17

Economic Instability

The markets will fall. Assets will crumble. Jobs will disappear. Discontent and fear will grow. Violence may appear inevitable. This type of thing has happened before. The truth of impermanence applies to economies as well as to everything else. Keep your head. Just as you should guard against becoming careless when things are going well, you should guard against carelessness amidst crisis. Perhaps you don't know exactly what's going on or how things will work out. But when did you ever really know? Certainty is an illusion. I am absolutely sure of it.

Fraught with Meaning

I applaud your ability to manufacture significance from vague and ambiguous language. It is because you *think* I'm talking to you that I *am* talking to you. Here's all I want to say to you today: Try to make friends with your deep, bitter regret. If you shower it with attention, it may tire of you and depart.

The Demon's Shattered Lens

Demons love to create mischief. A Danish sage once told me that long ago, at the beginning of the world, there was a demon who worked as an optical laboratory technician. This demon created a giant, diabolical lens that would distort the vision of every person in the world over the age of sixteen. The lens would make wholesome things look wicked, and wicked things look wholesome. The demon flew to the highest mountain where he planned to position the lens to filter the sun. But as he flew, the lens slipped from his grasp and shattered on the ground. A cloud of glass shards rose up and was carried all over the world by the wind. The particles of this ancient lens are very small, but they often get stuck in people's eyes. People can't feel the shard and don't even know that their vision has been distorted. They go around confusing what is wholesome and what is wicked. The only cure is to cry. Only a long, steady stream of sad, sad tears can wash away a shard of the demon's lens. It's generally true that if you've never wept desperately, you can't see properly.

JUNE 20

Better and Better

French psychologist Émile Coué suggested that his patients repeat the phrase: "Every day, in every way, I'm getting better and better." I am very sorry to inform you that Monsieur Coué is now little more than a historical footnote and a handful of dust. Your desire for self-improvement is admirable, but don't fool yourself. No amount of improvement will make you immortal.

June Solstice

Summer is finally here. Unless you live in the Southern Hemisphere, where it's now winter. What are you doing down there when you could be up here enjoying summer? Ah, the relativity of everything on the globe undermines my psycho logical need for absolutes. Although the world tilts and turns like a frenzied ballerina, you must find your own quiet center of gravity and try to stay on your feet.

JUNE 22

Specialness

Y ou're not special. Really, you're not. Take out the trash. Fold the laundry. Pay your bills. Life is meaningful as it is. You're cutting yourself off from everything genuine and useful when you insist on your specialness. A sense of specialness is a seed of resentment. Get over it.

JUNE 23

Acceptance

D o you love yourself? Can you express appreciation for yourself? When finally you can acknowledge yourself with humble gratitude, it will be a tremendous relief for others who endure your abusive tendencies, your careless ways, and perpetual, gnawing dissatisfaction. I for one am fed up.

JUNE 24

The Sullen Bride

Her wedding day was fast approaching and everyone was overjoyed, except for the sullen bride. Wedding gifts came from far and wide. A lavish honeymoon was planned. A weeklong feast was prepared at the palace. Everyone was happy, except for the sullen bride. Her bridesmaids bathed her with milk and honey and dressed her with the finest silk and gems, but the sullen bride still moped. "What is wrong?" asked the mother of the bride. "I can't help thinking," the bride sighed: "Someday, centuries from now, gay people will want to get married, too. That just ruins it for me." Need I point out the irrationality of this sentiment?

Arranging Your Mental Furniture

Your living room is arranged exactly the way you like it. Now suppose a guest drops in, moves your favorite chair, sits in it, and puts a damp glass on your favorite wooden table without even bothering to use a coaster. You might be taken aback, even though you had invited your friend to make himself at home. A similar thing can happen in conversation. Your precious notions are moved across the room. Someone carelessly leaves a ring on your wooden beliefs. You find this maddening, even though a conversation is an invitation to rearrange one's mental furniture. If a home is perfectly arranged with no blemish and nothing out of place, it's probably a show home. No one lives there.

Courage

You want my blessing for your marriage, but I'm afraid it will do you no good. My advice, like the advice of most holy sages, is purely theoretical and highly suspect, considering that I have never been married. In marriage, nothing will be the way you think it will be. Your likes and dislikes must soften. You must have courage to face whatever comes. It's likely that the whole thing will fall apart over an argument about in-laws, vegetarianism, or recycling. It happens.

No Blaming Allowed

As of today, you are no longer allowed to blame your voluntary actions on another person. "He made me lose my temper." "She made me falsify the bank statement." Not allowed. You are a grown adult. Man up. You too, ladies.

JUNE 28

Enough Is Enough

Aren't you sick of it? Aren't you full to bursting already? You gorge on food, on entertainment, on grievances, on sports memorabilia. You are filled to the gills with useless crap, yet you are starving. You are not nourished by what you consume because you consume delusion.

JUNE 29

Profit from Your Confusion

Many people have gotten rich by exploiting religious guilt and spiritual aspiration. So can you. Every time you think that someone else holds the key to your fulfillment or salvation, pay yourself thousands of dollars. But wait. That's crazy. Indeed. Paying yourself to help you become enlightened is just as crazy as paying someone else.

Pride

Once upon a time, a splendid lion grew up in captivity and was regarded as perfectly tame. A professional performer, he loved to wear feathers and sequins. He pretentiously dropped French phrases into everyday conversation and used more hairspray than necessary. Sadly, the tide of entertainment turned. Audiences regarded the lion's act as inhumane and antiquated. His agent dumped him. He was out on the street. People shook their heads in pity when they saw the humbled lion doing his mime routine in the park. One day a careless pedestrian stepped on the lion's paw. For the first time ever, the lion roared. He was as startled as the Sunday crowd, frozen with awe. Inadvertently he had found his voice and his primal nature. Soon he became a successful sports-team mascot. Point being, your true nature will emerge eventually—probably in response to crisis or adversity—regardless of your socialization and limited self-knowledge. Own it.

How the Dinosaur Made Friends

Mr. Tyrannosaurus was an enormous, scaled reptile with terrible claws and fearsome fangs. He had no friends. Everyone was afraid of him. He was sad and lonely. The dinosaur traveled to the Himalayas to consult a monk who was meditating in a cave. "Monk," he said, "I am quarrelsome. I rip others to shreds and eat them. How can I make people like me?" The monk explained that a radical makeover would take thousands of years. "If you want to change, you must make a commitment. It's all about nutrition and exercise." The monk put the dinosaur on a strict insects-only diet. He also prescribed a routine of yoga poses. The dinosaur did as he was told. Over time, he lost his taste for meat.

His teeth fell out and his mouth became beaklike to facilitate pecking at bugs. His rigorous yoga practice strengthened his arms. His scales softened into feathers. He lost a ton of weight. His fierce roar became a happy song. He became a colorful little songbird, beloved by all. Imagine what yoga and eating bugs could do for you.

Life's Not All Cupcakes and Daisies

You have done some good. You have accomplished and contributed. Now you must stop congratulating yourself about it. Wanting to be a better person does not give you bragging rights. If you are living fully, openly, and with awareness, you will endure times of paralyzing sorrow. You will wish that you never inquired into the meaning of life. There are no prizes for doing what you ought.

Martyrdom

Life is a crown of thorns that messes up your hair. Life is a veil of tears that doesn't match your gown. Life is a cross you bear that ruins your posture. Martyrdom doesn't look good on anyone.

Independence Day

Today I wave the flag and listen to the patriotic marches of John Philip Sousa—as brassy, bright, and rousing as America on a good day. Tonight I hope to enjoy a sky filled with fireworks. Dogs and small children have been known to panic at the sound of fireworks. They are not as sophisticated as we and, therefore, are not entertained by fiery explosions. Please keep in mind how frightening patriotism can be for the little ones.

Improved Technology

Perhaps you do not remember the invention of automobiles. I recall it vividly. People were thrilled that they would not have to depend on horses for transportation. Now, with automobiles we must depend on a finite supply of fossil fuels and worry about noxious emissions. Some people hope that these problems will be solved by the invention of cars that run on cleaner fuels. However, I suspect that improved technology is not the answer. Rather, we will merely trade known hazards for unforeseen hazards, again. Horse crap doesn't disappear. It just changes form.

JULY 6

You Can't Go Back

In my youth, I was fond of a cool, creamy orange beverage made by a shopkeeper in my town. Nowadays, I try to make my own drink with fresh-squeezed orange juice and a little milk, sugar, and vanilla. Sometimes I try adding frothy raw egg. No matter how I mix it, it doesn't taste the way I remember it tasting in the past. My dears, it is impossible to replicate a sensation to match one's nostalgia. It is foolish to try. You cannot step into the same river twice; time flows, changing everything. Now that I think of it, I haven't tried adding powdered vanilla pudding mix. Maybe that's the secret.

JULY 7

Living in the Now

Some gurus will tell you to live in the now. The present moment is all that matters. I disagree. "Embracing the sacred now" can be a hedonistic or nihilistic attitude thinly disguised as spirituality. Without the past, you're cutting off the wisdom of hard-won experience. Without a thought for the future, you cannot foresee the consequences of your actions. When you ignore your past and future, your "now" is foolish self-indulgence. But without the "now," retail sales would crash, and we can't have that.

All You Have Is Now

In the olden days, we had something called "movies," which were long strips of film comprising several thousand still images. Each image was called a "frame." By running these frames in rapid succession in front of a bright light and projecting them onto a screen, an illusion of movement was created. It looked as if people were walking and talking on screen, but really we were watching a series of snapshots. A moment of life is like a movie frame. It has meaning within the context of previous and subsequent frames. But each frame is a distinct, discrete opportunity to influence the story with a gesture, thought, feeling, or choice. Each frame is significant, contributing to a summer blockbuster or indie sleeper hit. To "embrace the now" means to appreciate the flicker of each momentary frame, knowing that it can make all the difference.

Courageous Wishing

If there's something you can do to help someone in distress, you should do it immediately. If not, you must wish for them to be helped immediately. For example, if someone is harming others, you can wish for that person to stop. You can wish for his or her victims to find safety. But let's be honest. Your wish will not fly through the air like fairy dust and resolve the situation. The person who benefits from this type of wish is you. Courageous wishing will help you develop a courageous heart. Alternatively, you could look at people in trouble and think, "Poor unfortunate ones. There's nothing I can do for them." This will foster a defeatist, cowardly disposition in you. Eventually, you will not be able to help even yourself.

Wishful Thinking

Wishful thinking is not the same as courageous wishing. Wishful thinkers believe
something to be true because they want it to be
true. Examples include believing that you can drink
yourself sober or spend your way out of debt. This
type of wishful thinking is obvious, but there is also
a sneaky variety. Being aware of the fallacy of wishful thinking, one assumes that because he or she
desires something to be true, it cannot possibly be
true. I want very much to believe in the goodness
of people. This is why I assume people are horrible.

Believe in Someone

What does it mean to believe in someone? Mostly, it means to be committed to that person's capacity for goodness and creation. It doesn't mean that you've chosen to ignore that person's dubious or dangerous qualities. It doesn't mean that you must suspend all rational and reasonable assessment of the person and just believe. No. Believing in someone does not mean buying his or her baloney. It means looking with a keen eye, listening with a perceptive ear, and scolding when necessary. Naturally, your efforts will be misunderstood by people who don't believe in you.

Self-Proclaimed Terrible People

I have known people who were an enormous dis-appointment to everyone who cared about them, and even to themselves. On the heels of self-created disaster, these people tend to say things such as: "I told you, I'm no good. Why do you expect any-thing but disappointment from me? I'm terrible." They have excused themselves from feeling remorse or shame because they have warned you of their horribleness. They will continue to break your heart. Proceed at your own risk. They risk noth-ing. Listen to them when they tell you they're rot-ten. They're not being ironic.

"Sometimes bullishness is stubborn refusal to face reality."

Self-Proclaimed Wonderful People

I question the self-evaluative skills of people who feel compelled to tell me how wonderful they are. Wonderful people usually don't boast about their personality traits. In fact, all too often, truly wonderful people hide their light under a bushel. A person who proclaims his or her wonderfulness is like a house for sale with a sign in the front yard that says, "I'm beautiful." Really? As if saying so will clinch the sale. People are going to make up their own minds about your wonderfulness regardless of what you tell them about yourself.

JULY 14

Wear Shoes

People are irritating. They just are. Plus, there are more of them than there are of you. So you have a choice. You can exhaust yourself trying to change everyone so they'll be less irritating, or you can develop a strategy for coping with irritation. You can become more patient or understanding, for example. You can learn to not take things personally. After all, you don't cover a rocky path with rubber. You merely put on shoes and hike in comfort. Some people are like sharp pieces of gravel inside your shoes, however, which ruins the analogy, the way they ruin everything.

A Sincere Offering of Gold

Once upon a time, a poor girl found a nugget of gold in a rocky stream. It became her prized possession. A few weeks later, an irresistibly charismatic preacher came to her town and announced that he was collecting precious metal to make a religious statue. The town folk gave him their rings and fancy silverware. The girl wanted to give the gold nugget. But the preacher refused her gift, saying she was too young to contribute. He melted down all the metal and poured it into a mold. But the statue came out dull and ugly. The preacher realized that only a sincere offering from a person of pure faith could make it shine. So he accepted the girl's gold, melted it, and the statue became beautiful. Cue the stirring music. This is exactly the type of story that an unscrupulous religious charlatan would invoke to take advantage of your sincere generosity. Don't be gullible.

JULY 16

Bless You

You cannot expect a spiritual leader to roll into town, bless you, and make your life meaningful. You must not slum around waiting for validation or absolution from a "holy person." You are the holy person. No one else can give you a blessing or take it away from you. And let me assure you, my stamp of approval won't be bestowed any time soon. Bless yourself.

A Humble Offering of Mud

Once upon a time, a great guru visited a small town. Townsfolk offered gifts to the guru to welcome him and honor his greatness. A poor little girl wanted to give the guru something, too, but she had nothing. So she made a mud pie. As she offered her gift, the townsfolk were mortified to see the girl give the guru a platter of filth. To their surprise, the guru bowed to the girl and thanked her. When you're enlightened, you see, it's the intention that counts, not the gift. This is why I emphasize to my students that I am certainly not enlightened in the least. They'll give me better stuff.

Not Funny

I'm troubled that young people today laugh at fart jokes. When did farting become crudely funny? During World War II, schoolchildren learned to fart in Morse code to help the war effort. It is said that Abraham Lincoln could fart a few bars of "Hail, Columbia," our first national anthem. Please honor this dignified history with your flatulence.

A Note on Etiquette

Have the decency to honk your flatulent outbursts into the public sphere, trumpeting their arrival so the rest of us can take evasive action. My great-grandfather once farted so hard he broke a window. He knew a thing or two about manners.

Summer Rain

I love when a sudden rainstorm breaks the heat of a sweltering day. Water is said to be a submissive element, taking the shape of the container that holds it, avoiding obstacles, following the path of least resistance. Yet, drop by drop it can wear away stone, and wave by wave it dissolves continents. Do not be surprised, then, that it has damaged your roof and established a rivulet down the wall of your closet.

Pacing Gets You Nowhere

A young man had a nagging feeling that he was missing an important opportunity. He paced the floor of his apartment, back and forth. "If only I had some direction, some sign," he thought. Just then, there was a knock on his door. Standing on his doorstep was the most beautiful woman he had ever seen. "Hello. I live downstairs," she said. The young man could not believe his luck. The woman of his dreams lived just downstairs. The woman said: "Your pacing footsteps echo in my apartment. Please stop." The man muttered an apology, and the woman returned to her apartment. Moral of the story: Good fortune might be right under your feet, but if you are morbidly indecisive, you will turn every stroke of luck against you. Get on with your life already.

Teachers and Their Parables

Throughout history, great sages have conveyed their teachings in the form of parables. These instructive vignettes are specific enough to make you think that they actually occurred, yet vague enough for you to adopt them as personal lessons. Many are subject to multiple interpretations. Some people find it maddening that their teachers did not come right out and state the truth plainly. You see, the purpose of a parable is to keep you from becoming rigid, dogmatic, and fixated on theory. It doesn't necessarily work, as Jesus and Buddha can tell you. But they'd find a roundabout way of saying it.

JULY 23

Weeding

I sat contentedly gazing at my garden. Then I saw a weed, spoiling my repose. You see, I look for weeds when I am dressed to do battle with them. I hunt them and pluck them all. Ah, it is only when we sit back to relax and enjoy the fruits of our labors that we see where we have missed a spot or two.

JULY 24

Eternal Sands

L ove is like a sand dune, shifting in the wind. When it gets in your underwear, it can be quite thrilling. However, sand has abrasive properties of which you should be aware. The most idiotic place to seduce someone is on a sandy beach. In theory, it's romantic, but in practice, it's unpleasantly gritty. I applaud your sentiment, but this is the worst date of my life.

There Is Always an Alternative

We had no choice. Our backs were against the wall. Our hands were tied." So often, it seems, business and government leaders claim that there is only one possible, acceptable course of action. My darlings, this is sophistry. There is always an alternative. Even if you are plummeting to earth with a parachute that won't open, don't resign yourself to saying good-bye. Try your backup chute. Try everything. Leadership entails being able to act skillfully and creatively in the face of difficulty. Yet we allow ourselves to be led by people who claim to be helpless. It's not surprising, then, that alternatives evaporate and hard impact becomes inevitable.

Toward Self-Sufficiency

Have no fear of economic disaster. Stockpiles of wealth can be erased in one Wall Street tick. It would not kill you to become resourceful. The crux of success is to take everything in your life—every scrap—and use it, wasting nothing. I am not telling you to forsake money and material comfort. I am warning you that you must not take these things for granted.

Law of the Jungle

A mouse lived under my kitchen cabinets. I imagined Mr. Mouse enjoying his residence, patrolling for tasty morsels and gleefully telling his friends about it, just as I would if I had rented a villa in the south of France. By attributing human, relatable characteristics to the mouse, I lost sight of what was really happening: a disgusting animal was piddling on my cookware and pooping in my crockery. In a fit of clarity, I killed Mr. Mouse with a trap, and I felt terrible. I would not have felt so bad if my cat had caught him. Isn't that interesting? I can see myself in the mouse, but not in the cat. We are a little bit of each—aren't we—both predator and prey. No need to be sentimental.

Still, I feel bad.

"We are a little bit of each—aren't we—both predator and prey."

JULY 28

Ditch the Raft

My words are like a raft to help you cross a river. Once you have crossed from the shore of delusion to the shore of awakening, there's no need for you to drag the raft around with you. Leave it for someone else and continue on your way.

JULY 29

Don't Freak Out

If you have burdens that you feel you cannot bear, this is a chance to become more supple and wise. Your situation is an opportunity for you to squeeze some creativity out of your dull brain. It is all part of the process of becoming lighter and brighter. If you want to wake up, you need a swift kick in the pants.

Heartbroken Tiger

The last wild tiger on earth is miserable. People have hunted his kind to the brink of extinction. He was once a sacred animal who shuttled gods and goddesses around Asia on his back. Symbolic of bravery and stealthy skill, tigers hide and sneak up on their prey. Sadly, the tiger's forests have been cleared. Without cover, the tiger can no longer hunt. In fact, fat bunny rabbits have been known to stand in the clear and taunt the tiger with rude gestures. Each day, the last wild tiger on earth watches from behind the last tree in the forest as lesser beings mock him. Have some respect for the bygone nobility of the jungle cat, even though he would eat you if he could.

Princess Arrow Rock

Long ago, a ferocious tiger killed the fiancé of a princess. After a period of bitter mourning, the princess grabbed her bow and arrows and went into the forest to slay the tiger. She could think of nothing but revenge. She walked far from the palace. The sun was setting. Suddenly, in the corner of her eye, she saw something move. Without thinking, she turned and shot, sinking her arrow into something massive. All was quiet and still. The princess went into the shadows to see what she had killed. To her astonishment, she found that her arrow had penetrated solid rock. She could not remove her arrow from the boulder, no matter how hard she tried. Point being, when your mind is focused in a life-or-death moment, the impossible becomes possible. Physical laws are suspended. But so what? She shot a rock. Try to do something more interesting with your life-or-death moment.

Preventive Maintenance

By taking care of little problems when they are small, you can keep them from becoming overwhelming. When you notice a bad habit creeping into your life, take charge and eradicate it immediately. Very quickly and quietly, a bad habit can take up residence in the vacant apartment of your mind. With each passing day that you don't evict it, the more comfortable it becomes. Each day, more and more willpower is required to resist. Be resolute from the start. Bad habits don't pay the rent.

Sleep Like a Child

I'm not getting enough sleep. When I do sleep, I do not sleep deeply. I envy small children who slumber peacefully while slumped awkwardly in a stroller. They can be lifted and carried with their heads lolling, limbs flopping, and they don't wake up. They sleep with perfect trust in their environment, yet they are fragile little beings. In everything, you should strive to conduct yourself as an adult. But you should sleep like a toddler.

"Trust in the goodness of others.
Sometimes."

Protection of the Seven-Headed Naga

When we think of guardian angels, we tend to regard them as friendly, gentle protectors made of diaphanous kindness. Actually, they're terrifying. You can't get a gig as a guardian angel unless you're touchy, mean-tempered, and intimidating. The seven-headed naga is perhaps the most exceptionally disturbing guardian. Think of a cobra with seven heads looking in every direction with the ability to travel underground, over water and through the air. It is the preferred protector of babies. So don't cross a baby. Most have deadly, fanged snake gods as backup.

Transactional Dating

A young friend complained that he had treated a young lady to an expensive dinner, but she did not reciprocate by having sex with him. He felt that she did not keep her side of the bargain. It is a common misconception that romance is an exchange of goods and services. Try to think of romance as a conversation. It requires two mutually interested parties who each have something to say, as well as the capacity to listen and respond. It is a voluntary, free communication. Who knows where it will lead? Save your money and work at becoming an inviting conversationalist. Also, trim your nostril hair.

Taunting Your Rivals

Why do you despise someone who is so similar to you? You could empathize with him or her quite easily. But empathy frightens you because it reminds you that you're just like everyone else. You're mortal and vulnerable. You fight this fact by convincing yourself you're better than that loser over there. You feel superior. You assert your superiority by mocking and jeering. This is the emotional mechanism underlying all heated sports-team rivalries. A baseball game is never just a baseball game. It's a laboratory of human psychology with hot dogs and beer.

Little Boy Blues

I am sorry to remind you that on this day in 1945, the United States dropped an atomic bomb nicknamed "Little Boy" on Hiroshima, Japan, thus unleashing horror on hundreds of thousands of people. And yet, the blast hastened the unconditional surrender of Japan's suicidal industrial war machine. Was the bomb good or bad? We'll set aside this question for ethicists and philosophers to debate. Today just remember that victory and defeat are dependent upon one another. The victors and the vanquished are forever united as two sides of the same coin. Victors hate hearing this.

AUGUST 7

What Do You Deserve?

When something bad happens to you, why do you assume you don't deserve it? Usually, when something good happens, you assume you deserve it. Why can't you understand that "deserve" has nothing to do with anything? No one ever gets what they deserve, good or bad. Justice is an ideal, not a functional reality.

A Dip in the Ocean

Hush up about being terrified of your brilliance. Do you ask, "Who am I to be so brilliant, gorgeous, talented, and fabulous?" No, not seriously. You ask, "Why don't others see how fabulous I am?" You pursue cosmetic surgery, life coaching, and image counseling to enhance how others perceive you. You're terrified of what others might think of you. You're terrified of criticism, failure, and loneliness. But let me tell you: I'm criticized, failed, and lonely all the time, and it's really not so bad. It's like stepping into the ocean. It can be a bit chilly at first, but once you dunk your head and become fully immersed, it's invigorating.

Like the Rain

Wisdom is like the rain, which falls equally on good and evil alike. It nourishes flowers as well as weeds. Some plants such as the cactus store water for later. Some plants grow rapidly but wither when the rains have passed. The rain is the same, but the nature and capacity of plants differ. This explains why some of my wise advice is absorbed and some is resisted, even though it's all from the same cloudburst. It's not me; it's you.

Too Positive

You chant positive mantras repeatedly, as if the universe can't hear you. You feel you must keep your mind occupied with obsessive positivity. Otherwise, if you utter the slightest negative word or formulate the smallest silent ugly thought, dark retribution will be unleashed upon you. Hmm. Heaven won't listen to an avalanche of your positive prayers, but it will respond swiftly to a single negative impulse? Perhaps you should put yourself in heaven's shoes. How annoying would it be if someone were to call on the phone or ring your doorbell incessantly until you answered? Heaven is obviously looking for a chance to mess with you.

I Worry about You

You are hungry for meaning. You long for that which is beneficial, true, and uncorrupted. These are the qualities of a brave seeker. Hooray. Still, I worry. I fear that your desire is so strong that it will compromise your powers of discernment. You will embrace partial truths thinking them to be great truths. You will embrace counterfeit teachers because they look almost like the real thing. You will see hints of falseness, but you will ignore them. Your intuition will whisper that you're being taken for a ride, but your desire will speak louder than your doubt. True teachers and teachings can withstand skepticism. Put up your dukes. You need to exercise spiritual self-defense.

AUGUST 12

Twaddle

Today you come grudgingly to your scolding. I resent this, but I understand. No one likes to be reminded of his or her inadequacy. Try harder today. Do better. Don't give me a lot of twaddle about how impossible your life is. Buck up.

AUGUST 13

Fortitude

Don't give up. Never give up. Even if I tell you to give up, don't. Somehow this will all work out. Hold on. Hold fast. Endure. The night is always darkest before dawn. There is a light at the end of the tunnel. Do not despair. Persevere. Look on the bright side. You may be tired, but the clichés are inexhaustible.

Keep Going

There will be times when you feel over-whelmed by the seeming futility of everything. There will be times when you cannot look on the bright side or even imagine that there is a bright side. I can do nothing to help you in such times. You must wander out of this barren wilderness on your own, like an emaciated survivor of an Antarctic expedition gone terribly awry. Somewhere a fire burns. A soft bed awaits you. Keep walking. If you give up now, you won't be able to sell the film rights.

Be Ready for Your Close-Up

If you come to me in your hour of need, I will pour you a cup of tea and ask that you please tuck in your shirt. Being troubled and woeful is no excuse for sloppiness. Clean up and put on your nice clothes. You'll be surprised how this boosts your mood. Wearing pajamas into the late afternoon will make you feel out of sorts. Brush your teeth. I want you to look presentable at the crucial moment. You will thank me when the cameras roll.

AUGUST 16

Apologize Once

Confess your transgressions and ask for mercy from the one you have wronged. But remember, you have only one chance to apologize. When you apologize for the second time for a repeat offense, your credibility will be damaged. Everyone will sense it. Your internal, intrinsic integrity will be compromised, not just other people's opinions of you. This explains the cold stares you've been getting from strangers.

AUGUST 17

Schadenfreude

There's a word for the malicious glee you feel when others are harmed: *Schadenfreude*, from the German—an elaborate puff pastry filled with sweet cream and cyanide. Don't indulge yourself no matter how tempting it may look.

Hobbies Versus Interests

Some people have hobbies, and other people have interests. These are two distinctly different kinds of people. People with hobbies are likely to ask others, "What do you do for fun?" For them, life is divided into "fun" and "not fun." People with interests, on the other hand, tend to become engrossed in whatever they happen to be doing. Performing a task is pleasurable in itself, even if other people—people with hobbies—would classify the task as "not fun." No one goes to the dentist for fun, but they're usually glad they went. Life is not intended to amuse you.

A Bad Influence

Someone who is bad for you does not waltz in and announce his toxicity. Rather, it's just the opposite. He is remarkably helpful, taking an interest in all your affairs. He will point out where your judgment is in error, especially regarding your own abilities. He will become indispensable as you realize you're less capable than you thought. You'll become convinced that he cares about you more than anyone. You'll even begin to question the loyalty of friends and family members who suggest that your new friend is a bad influence. As you gradually become more isolated, you'll find that his approval means a lot to you, yet he approves of you less and less. My dearest, this is how a bad influence undermines you: by being so coercively attentive yet hurtfully aloof that you no longer trust your own perceptions.

"Driven by aggression."

Summer of Burning Love

A h, summer is a wonderful time to catch your partner in an extracurricular love affair. You've seen the signs: a sudden interest in different music; unexplained changes in schedule; explanations or excuses that don't add up; a new habit of toting around a change of clothes; carrying a second mobile communications device that he or she thinks you don't know about. You can hire a private investigator to obtain photographic proof. But you know what's going on. You're in a burning house. You can get out, or you can stay in it. Maybe you'll want to rebuild later, after the house has burned to the ground. Right now, you need to avoid being crushed by a collapsing structure.

A Childhood Scolding

Once upon a time, a child was washing her hands. She built a rich lather of soap all the way up to her elbows. She was very proud of herself for washing so thoroughly. She looked up to see her father in the doorway. He shouted, "No." He told her to stop and to never do it again. The child began to cry. Many years later, the girl asked her father if he remembered the incident. He did. She asked, "But I don't understand why you scolded me for using too much soap." The man laughed. "Too much soap? I scolded you for washing your hands in the toilet bowl." The point: If you're going to take criticism to heart, make sure you understand what is being criticized.

A Narcissistic God

Some people highly revere their god, yet they have a dreadfully low opinion of themselves and others. They say, "My god is great, but I am nothing. You are nothing. Only my god is something." If I were this god, I would be insulted. I would wonder, "Why are you so ungenerous in your conception of me? Do you really think I want you to debase yourself and exalt me? Am I really an insufferable narcissist?" If I were this god, thus wounded, I would be tempted to mock, taunt, and rain plagues upon you. It explains a lot.

Religion Is Not Mandatory

Do you believe in a god or higher power? Do you think angels or spirits of your ancestors guide and protect you? That is all very well, but religion is not mandatory for a happy life. Worship if you must. But be aware that others regard your solemn beliefs as ridiculous fantasies. It is possible to be moral and ethical without religion, just as it's possible to be soaked in religion and still be unethical, immoral, and criminal. Those lawsuits are a sore subject for you, I know. But it's always the pious ones—the ones who speak often of their worship, sacrifice, and reverence—who aid and abet wrongdoing with their misplaced moral integrity.

AUGUST 24

Giving Me an Ulcer

You claim to be humble, but you think you're better than others because of your religion. Do you feel that your religion affords you status or privileges? If so, you have turned your religion into ugliness. Why must you take yourself so seriously? It is a burden to yourself and those around you. I say this out of friendship. Your inflated sense of importance is giving me an ulcer. Think what it's doing to your god.

The Glowing Hut

Once upon a time, a monk journeyed through the countryside. The sun was setting, and he was getting hungry. In the distance he saw a hut that seemed to glow, radiating joy. The monk hurried to the hut and knocked on the door. He was greeted by an old woman who welcomed him with delight. They ate and talked of many things. Finally, the monk asked if she had ever studied the great teachings. She confessed that she had met a teacher once who had taught her a mantra, which she had recited for years. Curious, the monk asked which mantra. She intoned it. "I know what you are trying to say," the monk laughed. "But you are pronouncing it all wrong. This is the correct way." He pronounced the mantra, thanked her for the meal, and continued on his journey. "It's lucky I was able to set her straight," the monk thought. If he had turned to look back, he would have seen that the hut no longer glowed. Know-it-all monks trample joy then pat themselves on the back. Jerks.

"Don't be a know-it-all."

AUGUST 26

A Punch in the Nose

Imagine that you are swimming in a warm, blue sea. A hungry beast rises from the deep and tries to take a bite out of you. In such a situation, you must deliver a swift punch to the beast's nose. Do not just float there and say, "Ah, I am a loving pacifist, so I must allow myself to be devoured by this beast of the deep." That would be stupid. You have an obligation to defend yourself against aggression. Of course, that's totally different than attacking someone whom you perceive to be a threat based on trumped-up intelligence reports. Sometimes, it's hard to tell whether you're in real peril or just really afraid. That's the frightening thing.

Remember

The world does not owe you a living. The world is not in love with you. The world is not a safe place. Do not idealize the world. Hope for the best, but prepare for the worst. Suffer what there is to suffer. Enjoy what there is to enjoy. Eat sensibly and exercise regularly. Be kind to animals. Be kind in general. Don't get all wigged out thinking you're Jesus or Holden Caulfield. You're not.

Escapist Overscheduling

A re you using the "I'm too busy" excuse again? Everyone can see right through it. You rush here and there to meet obligations. But there is a level of busyness that is laziness. Too busy to self-reflect? To listen to loved ones? To do what you truly want to do? Having the life you dream of takes hard, disciplined work. Busyness is a way of avoiding what is truly important. You're not fooling anyone. Plus, I'm hurt that you haven't returned my calls.

Gardens Grow

When I first planted my garden, I was afraid it would not grow. My shrub roses were frail. My clematis was fussy. Many plants withered and died despite my careful attention. A contorted filbert tree comes to mind; I could not save it from the summer heat. Now, my grounds are bursting with life. I find myself having to hack through dense shrubbery and cut back my flowering vines. It's almost too much growth for me to tame. When something takes root, it's as if it has a mind of its own, growing like mad. Be careful what you plant. Be selective. Once it takes root, it will own you.

Slacker Monkeys

One morning the Monkey Chief awoke from a bad dream. He rallied all the monkeys and announced it was time to harvest the mangoes. "You must remove all the mangoes from the trees," he said. "Pile them here. Otherwise, something terrible will happen." Most of the monkeys worked hard to gather every last mango. But two monkeys slacked off. "Nothing terrible is going to happen. Chief just wants us to work harder than necessary." During the night, one neglected mango fell in the river and floated downstream. A king taking his morning bath saw the mango. He ate it for breakfast. It was so delicious he wanted more. He led his army upstream. When they found the mango stockpile, they killed all the monkeys and took the mangoes. You don't always get a second chance to do a good job. Lives depend on attention to detail and a strong work ethic. Don't be a slacker monkey.

The Starfish Parable

A man was walking along a beach littered with thousands of starfish. He noticed another man picking up starfish one by one and throwing them back into the sea. "You'll never be able to throw enough of these starfish back to make a difference," said the first man. As the second man threw another, he said, "It makes a difference to that one." And, unbeknownst to him, it made a difference to the ecological balance of the offshore coral reef, which was being destroyed by predatory starfish. Don't second-guess Mother Nature.

The Scorpion and the Codependent Turtle

Once upon a time, a scorpion wanted to cross a river. He asked a turtle to let him ride on his back. "I'll take you across the river if you promise not to sting me." The scorpion promised, and off they went. When they reached the far shore, the scorpion stung the turtle. "Why did you do that?" the wounded turtle asked. "It's my nature," said the scorpion. Later, the scorpion wished to cross again. The turtle was still on the bank, smarting from his wound. "Hey, I'm sorry I hurt you earlier. I promise not to sting you if you carry me to the other bank." The turtle agreed. Just as before, the scorpion stung him. This went on every day for a week. Finally, a fish asked the turtle why he kept putting himself in a position to be stung. "You will never change the scorpion's nature," the fish said. "I know," the turtle said. "But his nature does not change my nature to be trusting, helpful, and forgiving." Crikey. Get away from those who can't stop harming you. Don't be a codependent turtle.

A Month of Oysters

Ah, at last: a month in which I can eat oysters. How I love their bright, briny taste. They filter nastiness and filth out of the water, yet they taste as fresh as a meadow. Some people mistakenly believe that a raw oyster should be swallowed whole, or else slathered with lemon juice and cocktail sauce to kill the taste. My darlings, if your oysters are so putrid that you must disguise their rot, you should not ingest them. Eat oysters only in months that have the letter *R* in their names, never in May, June, July, or August. You might be tempted to dismiss this as obsolete advice from an era without refrigeration, but don't. Oysters can transform mud into a delicacy. The least we can do in return is respect their privacy during their spawning season.

Make a Pearl

The oyster is ballyhooed by advice givers for its ability to turn irritation into a precious pearl. The oyster neutralizes an invading parasite or other irritant by covering it with layer upon layer of nacre, or mother of pearl, an iridescent sort of laminate. Perky optimists would have us be like the oyster and produce a luminous treasure by likewise coating our irritations with layers of forbearance. That's all well and good as a metaphor. I am reminded, however, that people do indeed create calcified nuggets such as gallstones and kidney stones. I wouldn't wish them on anyone, and I wouldn't want to wear them in a string around my neck. If you're going to make a pearl, please do so figuratively.

The Great Unknown

I'm not going to lie to you and say it's wonderful to die. Perhaps it is, but I do not know. Will you go to heaven? Be united with loved ones? Receive reward or endure punishment? I do not know. No one knows. Those who pretend to know are talking out their caboose.

"Death puts everything in perspective. My, what a lovely view."

Death Doesn't Make Appointments

Pretty stories about good or painless death may relieve your uncertainty and anxiety. Wishful thinking may help you to believe that death is not so bad, or that you have some control over when and how it will occur. You have no control. Give up your desire for control. It doesn't flatter you. Death is planning a surprise party for you. The surprise is the only fun part of death's otherwise crappy job.

The Ultimate Makeover

Stepping over the threshold of death requires the abandonment of every familiar thing that orients you in this life. Your eyes will no longer work. Your limbs will no longer move. Your thought processes, reliant as they are on the flow of blood and oxygen, will cease. Your memory will disintegrate. You will no longer be able to hear the voices of your loved ones. Soon your body will decay, leaving nothing but a handful of dust. You will fit into your skinny jeans, ah, but you will no longer care.

Live Your Life

It can be shocking to realize that everything you hold dear is transient, like shifting clouds or a small wave cresting at sea. Ultimately, it does not matter what happens when or after you die. How you live is more important. Yet you act as if life is an exercise in death avoidance. Perhaps it's time to organize your photo album.

Be Responsible

K nowing that you will one day die might spur you to accumulate irresponsible amounts of consumer debt. Why not take the luxury cruise, or buy the automobile you cannot afford? One day you'll be dead, so live it up. Do not use death as an excuse for meaningless extravagance. Of course, no one's going to stop you. There's no law against reckless hedonism *per se*. Okay, fine. Spend. Consume. Live it up. Your attitude is impenetrably childish.

A Flood of Scolding

Once upon a time, a thirsty man came upon a spring of sweet water flowing from a rock. He was parched, but he would not drink. A fellow traveler asked, "Your lips are dry, so why don't you drink?" The thirsty man replied, "Because there's no way I can drink it all." This is how you are. You cannot accept everything I say, so you reject it all. Drink what you want. Drink what you need. You don't have to drink the whole flood of wisdom to become hydrated. I'm not trying to drown you.

Cosmic Accountancy

Many people would like to believe there's some mechanism of cosmic justice that settles scores, like a stern accounts-receivable clerk who knows what is owed and by whom. You believe in cosmic justice because your whole conception of life is based on notions of reward and punishment. It's time to consider that there's no such thing as reward or punishment. There are no gold stars and no demerits. Just consider it.

Lesson of the Debtor King

Once upon a time, there was a debtor king who borrowed from a wise king and racked up enormous debt. "I have no choice but to incur these debts," he proclaimed. His people agreed because they had become accustomed to living beyond their means. Changing their lifestyle would be catastrophic. "We're passing this debt on to our children," they said, as if that were a mere abstract figure of speech. One day the wise king came to collect. The debtor king said, "We will pay you later. We have passed the debt on to our children." Hearing this, the wise king sent his army to conscript all the children and march them far away to work in his salt mines. "This is an outrage," the debtor king protested. "You stole our children." The wise king countered, "Any king who would use his children as collateral is not fit to raise them. You have enslaved them, not I." Quite so.

Three Thugs

One day a monk was walking down a city street when he was confronted by a group of thugs. They shoved the monk to the ground. The monk began to cry. The thugs laughed and made fun of the monk's cowardice. "I am not afraid of you," the monk said, rising to his feet. "I am sad for you. You are young and strong. You could help people and do good works. Instead, you go around hurting people. I am sad because I know how bitterly you will regret your actions one day." The thugs had never seen anyone shed tears on their behalf. Two of them were so moved that they decided to stop being thugs. But the third thug blew the monk's brains out, and they all went to jail. There are no winners in this story, no upside to thuggery.

Your Personal Trainers

Do not be surprised when the people with whom you must associate are not nice to you. It is not their job to be nice to you. It is their job to prey on your insecurities and make you face your weaknesses. People who are not nice are the ones who can show you what is blocking your happy liberation. It is their duty to incite your rage. They give you a chance to exercise your compassion and wisdom. Antagonists are not enemies. They are like workout partners or jogging buddies for your good nature.

Take a Stand

Why must you smooth everything over? Why are you afraid of disagreement, heated discussion, and people threatening to cancel their subscriptions? You gloss over thorny issues instead of dealing with them forthrightly. The more you do this, the more resentment seethes in others. Do not be such a mediocre mealy mouth. Stand up for something.

SEPTEMBER 15

Leaning Too Far in Any Direction

When people see a falling fence or teetering rock, they can't resist pushing on it. If it looks as if you might fall, people are all too happy to give you a shove. Don't lean too far in any direction. Stay upright and everyone will respect you. No, they probably won't respect you. Why should they? But they are more likely to leave you alone. That's the best you can hope for.

SEPTEMBER 16

Feet on the Floor

Your feet belong on the floor. This is the natural order of things. You upset the natural order when you sit with your feet up on a desk, table, or chair. This makes you look slovenly and also invites misfortune. Sit up straight. Pay attention. There will be a test.

SEPTEMBER 17

Costly Investment

You wish to turn one dollar into one million dollars. We all understand this desire. But do not play games of chance. True wealth results from diligence and hard work. There are no shortcuts. Do not invest one cent in the false belief that you can get something for nothing. You can't afford it.

SEPTEMBER 18

Step by Step

How do you eat an elephant? One bite at a time. How do you pluck a goose? One feather at a time. How do you build a fortune? One dollar at a time. Do not waste your money on trifles. Put aside a small portion in savings each week. Your fortune will grow little by little. I despair when I think how much you squander on novelty beverages and hair styling products.

Awaken Your Conscience

When I urge you to apply yourself, you roll your eyes. When I say you are lazy, you dismiss my insightfulness as mere name-calling. Your own conscience should be chiding you. Your own conscience should tell you the things I'm telling you. Your conscience is dangerously asleep, like a slumbering infant in a burning house or a senator after a long day of golf and strippers.

The Purpose of Desire

Desire is like the burning firewood of life, without which there would be no light and no
heat. You will not necessarily get what you want.
Obstacles, disappointment, and failure are like a set of
fireplace tools, which poke and prod your desire to
burn more intensely. In the end, ashes are all that will
remain. Whether you were able to fulfill your desire
is irrelevant. What matters is whether your desire
provided warmth and illumination in your life.

Learn to Suffer

When you feel like crap, just remember that things could be worse. When you're on top of the world, remember there is no such place. Not very comforting, I know. We are not supposed to be comfortable. We are supposed to dwell boldly in the crap of this world and not be defeated. If you want to be happy, you must learn how to suffer without it killing you.

You Make a Difference

When you mope or act like a know-it-all you bring everyone down. Nobody likes a sour-puss. Nobody admires someone who continually asserts his or her expertise or credentials. Just be natural. Be yourself. I am not going to tell you to smile. Do what you feel is right for you. You will bring others peace and happiness when you discover the joy that is inside you this very moment. People notice you. You do make a difference, if only by negative example.

SEPTEMBER 23

Yes, You Have a Dark Side

I would be fibbing if I claimed that all people are sweet and lovely as chocolate chiffon pie. Do not be astonished by the intractable malice you encounter in some people. We have our better selves, which are better than we can fathom. We also have our worse selves, which are dark and destructive indeed. Sadly, disturbed losers abound. It is your duty to avoid becoming one yourself.

SEPTEMBER 24

Obscenity

When I was a girl, men found a glimpse of a woman's ankle to be titillating. Today, eroticism is little more than debasement and violence. A famous jurist once remarked that one knows obscenity when one sees it. Sadly, we see it so often that we no longer recognize it.

SEPTEMBER 25

Love and Lover

An impediment to getting over Your Ex is thinking that "love" and "lover" are inextricably linked. Many people mistakenly believe that one exists because of the other. When their lover leaves, they believe love is gone, too. Not so. Love is not dependent on Your Ex. You still have love, even if you feel loveless and unlovable. Feelings are rarely a good measure of what's really going on. It's usually when you feel your worst that you're becoming a more tolerable person.

Looking for Direction

When you're feeling low, you might be tempted to look for mystical signs and answers. This is dangerous. You might stumble upon an ex-lover and assume it's more than a coincidence and that the universe is telling you to get back together. An investment scheme seems like the timely answer to your financial troubles. An invitation to join a new religion or social movement seems heaven sent. You cannot foist responsibility for your choices on the universe or a deity because of a so-called sign. You can't say, "Heaven wants me to do this," as if you have no choice. You do have a choice. You feel a void and want solace. You're looking for rescue. You will find it because you want to find it, not because it is an intelligent or helpful response to your problem.

Failed Prophecy

Once upon a time, a charismatic guru warned that the world would be flooded and everyone would die. Only a group of chosen people would be able to escape. He told everyone who was interested in being saved to quit their jobs, sell all their stuff, and work for him on a remote farm. The day the flood was to come, the guru herded everyone into a pasture to await the arrival of a spaceship that would rescue them. The group waited. No spaceship. No flood. After that, instead of sheepishly admitting they had been conned, many members of the group believed the guru's new spin: their prayers had saved the world. As a general rule, the more time, money, and belief you invest in something, the stronger your need to justify your investment. Be on guard.

Quick Profits

Two poor men were in the woods chopping firewood to sell. They came upon a tall tree filled with fruit. A piece of fruit had fallen on the ground. The men ate it and found it uncommonly delicious. They realized that they could sell it for a good price in the market. "But the tree is too tall for us to reach the fruit," one man said. The other suggested that they chop it down. So they did. They sold the fruit and made a lot of money. The following year, they were broke again, and they had killed their magic fruit tree—thus illustrating the stupidity of focusing only on quick profits. Stop it.

Disillusionment

You want answers, but there are only more questions. You want security, but you are increasingly vulnerable. Things aren't going your way. You feel disillusioned and disappointed. Disappointment is a sign that magical thinking is losing its stranglehold on your life. Always may you be disappointed.

Walking on Water

A man invited a woman to a lakeside picnic on a warm fall day. He wished to impress her with his supernatural powers. "I will show you something amazing," he said. "It took me twenty years of meditative discipline to learn this." He stepped on the surface of the lake and walked all the way to the other side. Seeing this, the woman climbed in a rowboat and rowed to the opposite shore. "It took me about five minutes to learn how to do that, and here we are at the same place." Women can be inexplicably hard to impress. If you're going to acquire a supernatural skill, learn something useful and hip like teleportation.

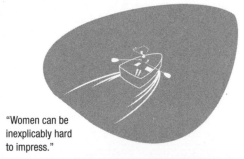

"Women can be inexplicably hard to impress."

OCTOBER 1

Live and Let Live

Don't worry if people hate you. They'll survive, and so will you. All is well. All is peaceful. How I make myself laugh sometimes.

OCTOBER 2

The Nature of Evil

Evil is a lack of conscience, just as cold is a lack of warmth. Deficits in conscience tend to shift over time. For example, Americans used to be repulsed by the thought of private companies profiting from war. It was seen as unpatriotic; some people even likened it to treason. Today, there's no social shame in profiteering. Guard your conscience. It's like fluffy insulation in your attic, and the only true bulwark against evil.

Marauding Magpies

I used to think that neighborhood children were throwing bagels into my trees. I would see bagels wedged between branches, and I would wonder. Soon, I discovered that the squirrels were ingeniously salvaging bagels from the trash of a nearby coffee shop. When my trees were festooned with breakfast pastries, marauding magpies descended, stealing the squirrels' stash. All their labor and supplies were taken from them in a single afternoon. Perhaps it goes to show that the old ways are best; better to bury your nuts than to display them. For survival, nature advises us to modestly and discreetly put up our stores.

A Month of Monsters

What frightens me most? People who form relationships based on calculation. People whose brains sort through emotions in the same way they would solve a math problem. People who are fluent in the vocabulary of love but do not love. Such people are more common than you might suppose. If you have a conscience, congratulations; not everyone does.

A Haunting Month

It's hard to prove or disprove the existence of ghosts, but people tend to be frightened of them anyway. At the same time, people don't seem particularly frightened by the evident horrors of frantic consumption, speculative bubbles, and complex financial instruments that can crash the global economy. Mysterious supernatural specters are always more terrifying than the screamingly obvious ones.

Third Time's a Charm

I'll allow someone to lie to me three times before I withdraw my trust. For some people, one lie is enough to destroy a relationship. I'll allow three because most of us tell little fibs for innocent reasons, or because we can't remember details. But three lies—significant lies—is my limit. One of my friends has a five-lie limit, thankfully, which is why we are still friends. I'm on lie four with her. It's important to set a limit on how much dishonesty you'll tolerate in your relationships. Stick to it.

OCTOBER 7

A Beautiful Night for Gaslight

If someone wanted to drive you crazy, he or she would constantly deny your perceptions. You would observe, "My dear, you seem oddly distant." He or she would respond, "How strange of you to say that. I was just thinking that *you* seem oddly distant. You're not yourself, somehow. Frankly, I'm worried about you." Perhaps you think such manipulation would be laughably transparent to you. Not so, my darlings. Rather, I fear you are going mad.

OCTOBER 8

Be Suspicious of Flattery

Your desire to be liked and appreciated makes you vulnerable to flattery. How charming. How utterly winning that someone you hardly know has lavished you with compliments or humbly confessed complete admiration. Watch out. You're off balance. You're wonderful, but not that wonderful.

OCTOBER 9

Don't Confuse Fear
with Respect

Some people hold positions of influence and power, yet they are little more than bullies. They spread misinformation in an attempt to ruin the reputations of those who oppose them. They use threats of economic reprisal or physical violence to make people think twice about challenging their will. And I'm just talking about the ladies in my canasta club.

Do You Love Yourself?

A young friend came to me in a troubled state. His girlfriend had accused him of being too in love with himself to ever be in love with her. "It's not true," he said vehemently. "I constantly feel defective. I feel that I'll never measure up. That's why I need her to bolster my ego. If I loved myself, I wouldn't have to get my self-esteem from putting her down." Quite so. Unfortunately, people who despise themselves are never self-aware enough to admit their toxic effect on others. In fact, I made the whole thing up. My young friend said no such thing.

Charity

Once upon a time, a woman was asked to donate some of her household goods to help the poor. Her husband made a large pile of items to give away. Seeing the pile, the woman was not happy. She examined the items and announced that she did not want to part with any of them. She asked her husband, "If I give away all of this, what is left for me to keep?" Her husband countered, "If you keep all this, what is left for you to give?" This is an excellent attitude, except when you're giving blood.

Beware Pity

Most people don't want to be pitied. Trustworthy people have their pride, even in difficult circumstances. They will accept charity if necessary, but they don't need you to feel sorry for them or treat them as if they are incapable. Beware those who play on your sympathy and court your pity. Smart cons know they can get away with almost anything as long as people feel sorry for them. Leave pity to the saints, and keep an eye on your pocketbook.

Demonic Relativity

Once upon a time, a monk vowed to rid a haunted house of a fierce demon. Little did he know, a real-estate executive vowed to accomplish the same task on the same night. The monk arrived first and waited inside until nightfall. After dark, the executive arrived. The monk, mistaking the executive for the demon, would not let him in the house. The executive, mistaking the monk for the demon, fought ever harder to enter. Their battle raged until dawn, with both men hollering, slamming doors, and repelling each other. In the morning light, they quickly discovered that they were each fighting a demon of their own making. They fell in love, bought the house, and lived in it happily ever after.

Trading One Illusion for Another

Once upon a time, a young man saw gold glittering in a stream. He jumped in the water and tried in vain to find the nugget. He gazed into the water, but he could no longer see the gold. The next day in the same spot, the man again saw the gold. He jumped in the water and searched but could not find it. A passerby asked what he was doing. "I keep seeing gold in the stream, but when I search for it, I can't find it." The passerby pointed at a house of worship on a nearby hill and said, "My boy, what you're seeing is the reflection of that gold ornament on top of the holy shrine. That is where you should seek true riches in this life." Chagrined, the young man renounced worldly wealth and embraced religion. After all, he was sweet but not very bright.

OCTOBER 15

Cultivate Boredom

Your whirlwind of busyness gives your life meaning. You must always be doing something or consuming new information. My darlings, boredom is not your enemy. Boredom is the best thing that can happen. Pure boredom strips away all distractions and stories you tell yourself. You're left with just you—lovely, unpretentious you. Sadly, you engage in an orgy of aimless online twiddling to avoid meeting this person.

Forces of Nature Compete

Once upon a time, two forces of nature squared off in a competition to remove the coat from a man's back. The cold wind blasted the man with gusts, but the man held stubbornly to his coat. Next, the sun took its turn. It shined pleasantly upon the man, warming him. Soon, he gladly took off his coat. There are times when cold, furious blasts can't get results, but sustained warmth will do the trick, especially if you want someone to disrobe.

OCTOBER 17

Spare Me

Spare me your insincere, self-conscious apologies. Whether you incessantly chide yourself or pat yourself on the back, either way you are self-centered. Self-loathing is just as indulgent as self-congratulation. It is a sneaky way of fixating on yourself with pride. Your constant, self-effacing interjections are just as grating as another person's incessant boasts. Please stop.

Timing Is Crucial

Once upon a time, a wealthy man had attendants for everything. When the man passed gas, he had a special attendant fan his buttocks to rapidly dissipate the odor. When the man carelessly dropped a cigarette butt, he had a special attendant grind it into the pavement. One day, as the wealthy man smoked a cigarette, an ambitious attendant kicked him in the mouth and knocked him unconscious. Everyone was stunned. "I wanted to impress him by being the first to stamp out his cigarette," the attendant said. Timing is everything. Also, competing for a promotion in a perverse, soul-killing workplace will prompt you to do regrettable things.

OCTOBER 19

Blissfully Above It All

I have a young friend who claims that suffering is optional. If you have the right attitude—if you can frame your circumstances in the right way—you need not feel pain or distress. If you lose someone dear to you, oh well. He or she is in a better place, and so are you. If calamity befalls you or your loved ones, oh well. That's how it goes. No need to feel sorrow or remorse. My friend calls this attitude "equanimity," and he's quite proud of having "achieved" it. I tell him he sounds like a perfect psychopath. Sadly, he thinks I'm joking. Don't trust anyone who claims to be above ordinary human feeling.

Lack of Empathy

You're guided by an inner sense of right and wrong, taking into account the feelings of others, I hope. You are capable of empathy—of identifying with others. Some people do not have this ability. No amount of your being nice, or mean, will change them. They were born that way. Because you are empathetic, you will argue and disagree. This is where your empathy fails: Try as you might, you cannot imagine what it's like to be unable to empathize. You just can't do it. It's a conundrum. Believe me when I tell you.

Something's Missing

For centuries, sailors on long ocean voyages came down with a horrible disease. Their gums would turn spongy, and their teeth would fall out. They would bleed and die for no apparent reason. Eventually, people learned that the disease—which we call scurvy—could be cured by eating citrus fruits or other substances high in vitamin C. The disease is caused not by the presence of a germ, but by the absence of a vital nutrient. Perhaps you suffer from spiritual scurvy. What you have isn't the problem. Rather, you suffer from what you lack: Empathy. Maturity. Humility. You get my drift.

Puppy Proxy People

Who doesn't love dogs in public places? Especially dogs who jump up or nuzzle the crotches of strangers, dogs who are free to roam and slobber and poop as their owners reassure everyone, "It's okay. He's friendly." Who doesn't love that? I don't, of course, but I can't hold it against the dogs. I used to think their owners were good-naturedly oblivious to leash laws and normal social boundaries. Now I'm not so sure. I think many people use their dogs as proxies to act out their own antisocial impulses. People cannot disregard the rights and boundaries of others with impunity, but their dogs can and do. No treat for you.

Carving a Monument

Once upon a time, a young sculptor found a splendid, mountainous boulder in the forest. He vowed to carve his masterwork from it. For years, he blasted, chiseled, and whittled away at the stone. He had no idea what he was crafting. Many decades later, at the end of his life, the sculptor emerged from the forest with his masterwork: a tiny pony carved from a mighty mountain. My darlings, life is like an immense canvas or splendid boulder. You are the artist. It would be nice if you had a vision for your masterwork, a vision to match the size of your canvas. It's a shame to turn something so grand into something so small.

Outsmarting the Tiger

L ong ago in a village nestled deep in the jungle, people were being eaten by the local tiger at an alarming rate. In each case, the circumstances were the same: A villager walking through the jungle was attacked from behind by the tiger. The villagers tried going into the jungle in pairs or small groups, but that did not stop the tiger. One day a villager strapped a mask to the back of his head in hope of confusing the tiger. It worked. Soon, the tiger had no clue whether the villagers were coming or going because they all had two faces. To outwit a predator, sometimes you have to wear a mask.

No Shame in Guilt

You should feel guilty, but you should not feel ashamed. Guilt is the natural response to having done something wrong, hurtful, or foolish. Shame is the corrosive belief that you are a bad person. You are exceedingly difficult and frequently unpleasant, but it is unlikely that you are a bad person. Please try to feel more guilt. Leave shame to the basest criminals, who, ironically, are least likely to feel ashamed.

Guilt Is Good

Would you intentionally put your hand on a hot stove? No, you would not. If you were to inadvertently touch a hot burner, you'd pull your hand away. Guilt involves a similar reflex. If you felt no sense of obligation toward others, or toward your personal values, you would not feel guilty. Guilt lets you know when you have transgressed a boundary that is important to you. Guilt is like the carbon monoxide detector for your good nature. Poison! Alert.

Being Manipulated by Guilt Is Bad

When someone puts a guilt trip on you, your internal alarm should sound. People who play on your sense of guilt are trying to manipulate you for their own purposes. Likely, they are inflating your responsibility while minimizing or denying their own. This is what gives guilt a bad name. You should learn how to recognize and honor your guilt when it arises naturally—so you'll know the difference between honest guilt and trumped-up guilt incited by someone else. People who have never felt a pang of honest guilt in their lives are usually masters of manipulation. Don't let them mess with your head.

Obedience to Authority

Turns out, we all tend to be obedient to authority. Studies demonstrate that most of us will follow the commands of a person deemed to be an authority—a doctor, law-enforcement officer, or game-show host—even if we know that our actions are inflicting pain on another person. Somehow, we believe that following authority absolves us from individual responsibility. Or we think that harming others at the behest of authority is the right thing to do. It's funny that we fear ghosts and goblins when we ourselves are so terrifying.

About Halloween Costumes

Wearing a Halloween costume is an adorable way for a child to play make-believe. When adults don costumes, however, the custom grows darker. A disguise offers an excuse to indulge an otherwise inappropriate fantasy, or to do things you would not ordinarily do. I know a man who gutted a freshly killed deer and wore the carcass as a costume, going from door to door to frighten the neighborhood ladies, including me. Halloween has devolved from a festival honoring the dead into a celebration of horror and cruelty in the dubious name of fun. No wonder our nerves are shot and we can't stop eating tiny candy bars.

OCTOBER 30

Vampires and Werewolves

Young people today find vampires and werewolves appealing. Boys want to be them; girls want to fall in love with them. When I was a girl, vampires and werewolves were commonplace in real life, and we preferred to avoid them. Back then, it wasn't fashionable for a woman to develop a suicidal attraction toward a bloodsucker or wild flesh-shredder. Ah, the good old days, when we didn't romanticize parasitic, abusive boyfriends.

Trick or Treat

Each year, dozens of children come to my door asking for candy. One year I felt guilty about doling out sweets to youngsters and potentially damaging their dental health. So I decided to distribute tubs of organic yogurt full of calcium and beneficial probiotics. I could see by the looks on the children's faces that "trick or treat" had turned from a spirited demand into a perplexing question. *Yogurt? Really?* I learned my lesson. Now I give out fistfuls of sweets. Let children have their small joys. Don't be a nutrition scold on Halloween.

Leave the Leaves

Leaves come and go, while the sturdy trunk and branches of the tree remain. It's not as if leaves are inconsequential. They're papery little work-horses, converting sunlight into nourishment. Then they fall, becoming mulch, which breaks down into soil. Leaves change until they no longer resemble leaves, yet their influence never ceases. They no longer exist, but they still exist—in my yard, especially, since I don't rake and dispose of them properly. It would be wrong to interrupt the natural decay of leaves, the circle of life, and the wonderful paradox of impermanence, don't you think? My lower back twitches with agony if I even think about trying.

NOVEMBER 2

Like Enlisting in the Military

If you can't restrain yourself from rushing into a romantic relationship, behave as if you have enlisted in the military. Make a total commitment for a set period of time—in your case, two years. Brace yourself for a taxing boot-camp environment of endless obstacles. You must give your all each day with no reward or acknowledgment. Discomfort and doubt will be your constant companions. You will get blisters. There will be no champagne. Do your time. Serve honorably. If you both approach your affair with such a serious attitude, your union has a chance of success. It's a partnership, after all, not a pleasure cruise.

Descending into Fakeness

When did we decide that fakeness is just as good as reality, if not better? From fake breasts to online virtual environments, artifice supplants authenticity. Las Vegas hotels simulate European cities. In India, a manufactured snow park features a fake climate with fake bears. Simple amusement parks have become immersive illusion destinations. What is this crap? When your whole culture goes mad, where does that leave you?

NOVEMBER 4

Change Isn't Everything

You are willing to obliterate your supposedly undesirable characteristics in the hope of becoming a better person. I'm not going to congratulate you for that. Before embarking on a quest to change yourself, first get to know and understand yourself. Not all change is for the better. Just be yourself—only more so.

NOVEMBER 5

My Snare Is Set

I am always right, and you are always wrong. Once you become my follower, you are my follower forever. You become a spiritual child, permanently infantilized. My way is the only way. If you ever break with me, you will fall into a hell of incessant suffering. To distract you from these truths, I flatter you. I insist that you are a chosen one, a person of rare virtue and insight. My other converts will gush about how magical their lives have become since I enthralled them. You will feel very special and lucky. This is how I trap you with mink-lined shackles of your own self-doubt.

The Eyeball Demon

One day a demon heard a spiritual practitioner boasting of his newfound wisdom. To teach him a lesson, the demon transformed himself into a blind man and approached the seeker. "You are spiritually gifted," the demon said. "But you lack a tiny bit of wisdom. I can give it to you, but first you must do something for me." The demon asked for an eyeball. "You have two good eyes, and I have none," the demon explained. "Giving me one of yours would be an act of compassion." Convinced, the seeker gave up one of his eyeballs. The demon dropped it in the dirt and squashed it under his foot. Ouch. Everyone has something to teach, but sometimes the price is too high.

Glorifying Mistreatment

Some gurus say that it is beneficial to be treated poorly. When someone is discourteous to you, you learn the value of courtesy. When someone is spiteful toward you, you learn the ugliness of grudges. When someone takes advantage of you, you learn how wrong it is. This is poppycock. When treated poorly, people tend to treat others poorly. Gurus who extol the benefits of being treated poorly usually treat people like crap. They rationalize their bad behavior by trying to convince you they're doing you a favor. I'm insufferable, but at least I serve you punch and dainties as I shatter your dreams.

NOVEMBER 8

Exchange Places

When someone treats you in a proud or condescending way, you hate it. It does you no good, however, to waste time and energy stewing about the arrogance of others. Rather, try putting yourself in their place. If you were as wealthy, powerful, gorgeous, talented, educated, intelligent or whatever as they are, would you feel superior? Of course you would. In fact, you would be offensively scornful. You would be even more scornful toward people who resented your superiority. So don't hate the arrogant. Be understanding and patient with them, as you would want them to treat you if you were a preening ass.

Put Your Imagination to Good Use

Imagine that you are in another person's circumstances. What would it be like to swap places with him or her? If you're feeling bold, imagine for a moment that you two are the same person—what harms him, harms you; what helps him, helps you. If just a fraction of your fantasy life were devoted to this exercise, you would quickly become more emotionally fit, toned, and sculpted. Instead, you keep practicing your award-acceptance speech. Your empathy wastes away like an unused limb as you thank the Academy.

Be Like the Squirrel

Squirrels bury acorns all over my yard, yet I don't have the good sense to keep a few cans of soup in my cupboard. Back in the day, when I had to claw my subsistence out of the ground, I was better prepared and more resourceful. Now, like most Americans, I am spoiled by the speedy delivery service of my neighborhood Asian bistro. Even rodents plan for lean times. You have no excuse not to. When the apocalypse comes, you'll wish you had stocked up on toilet paper.

"Even rodents plan for lean times. You have no excuse not to."

Compassion Stings

Compassion is not the same as niceness or politeness. Sometimes compassion is harsh to the ear, like the voice of a parent telling a child not to run blindly into the street. Sometimes compassion is like the sting of antiseptic on a wound. Sometimes compassion is a sharp sword to cut through delusion. You can't be compassionate if you don't have the courage to be unpleasant.

NOVEMBER 12

Accept but Don't Concede

By all means, accept who you are. Accept the circumstances of your life. Receive your responsibility. But don't confuse acceptance with concession or surrender. Don't just give up and paint a happy face on a crappy situation. Acceptance means acknowledging what you have to work with and where you actually are. It's like a starting block, the point from which you begin. Go.

Wanting to Be Happy

You want to be happy, and you don't want to suffer. But in pursuing happiness and avoiding suffering, you muck it up. You spend lavishly in pursuit of happiness. You find yourself in debt, which you repackage and defer in an effort to avoid pain. Next thing you know, whole countries are declaring bankruptcy. You chase happiness and run from suffering like a headless chicken. This is expensive. Learn how to be still.

Wanting to Be Loved

You want to love and be loved in return. But you can't stop screwing it up. You pursue those who don't return your affection. You are indifferent toward those who care for you. You're fickle in your tastes, falling in and out of love like a stumbling drunkard. Learn how to love without an object. Do not be the object of love. Do not project your love at an object. Love as if you are a radiant sun, burning impartially. Don't ask what it means, just do.

You Want to Be Entertained

You say you want to be happy but, really, you want to be entertained. You want to forget about yourself for a while, to lose yourself in amusement and intoxication. There is no greater white-knuckle thrill ride than your life, yet you would rather drive fast and recklessly for so-called fun. This is escapism, of course, not happiness. Happiness is when you reach the terrifying peak of your life, and in the moment before the inevitable, stomach-churning, downward plunge, you can look around and say, "My, what a lovely view."

Happiness and Satisfaction

When you are dissatisfied, you are unhappy. You think satisfaction equals happiness. Yet you always want things to be different than they are. You exhaust yourself trying to adjust your environment to conform to your wishes. You think that when you finally succeed, you will be satisfied and happy at last. But there is no end to your dissatisfaction because nothing remains permanently perfect. If you want to be happy, you must learn how to be dissatisfied without it ruining your day.

Praise and Blame

You enjoy being praised, but you fear being blamed. The underlying phenomenon is the same in either case: You are being singled out and held responsible. Is it true what they're saying? Are you responsible? Just a few days ago, you were practicing your award-acceptance speech, thanking everyone who helped you. You could not have accomplished anything by yourself in a vacuum. You are only partially responsible at best—or worst. You crave praise and reject blame, even though both are based on the flawed premise that everything is within your power. It is not.

Praise Hog or Scapegoat

Some people insist on being celebrated and praised. They thirst for compliments and accolades because they are fragile and insecure. Equally annoying are people who blame others every time something goes wrong. Sadly, some people actually believe they are always to blame. They, too, are fragile and insecure. Do you see how praise and blame can be taken to extremes, warping personalities? They are the same force. One is called a hurricane; the other is called a typhoon. Both can wreck your little island.

Drinking the Kool-Aid

You don't think it could happen to you, do you? You're too smart to get involved in a cartoonish cult. You would never revere a homicidal maniac, drink poison, and die in an erstwhile utopian colony in a distant jungle. No one joins a cult. Rather, they band together with like-minded people to achieve noble goals under the guidance of a charismatic leader whom they trust implicitly. No one thinks it's a cult when they join. But then they're systematically deceived and emotionally manipulated. Republicans and Democrats, I'm talking to you.

Embrace Negativity

There's nothing wrong with negativity. In math, for instance, multiplying two negatives results in a positive. This sounds illogical and counterintuitive, perhaps. It sounds like, "Two wrongs make a right." See what you're doing? You judge "negative" to have moral value, representing harm or deprivation. But its value is determined by how you choose to use it. Negativity itself isn't a problem. Your negativity about negativity, however, has turned you into a fool in a rowboat with one oar in the water. You can't understand why you're spinning in circles. Pull the other oar.

Embrace Anger

You have every reason to be angry. You didn't get what you expected. Something needs to change. Maybe you need to take steps to protect yourself from further harm. Then again, maybe you need to develop more realistic expectations. Regardless, it's okay to be angry. In fact, people who tell others not to be angry really cram the biscuits down my craw.

Just Anger Is No Justification

You don't have to justify your anger to me or to anyone. But remember: Being angry doesn't give you a free pass to abuse someone, not even yourself. Justified anger does not justify your actions, your addictions, or your foreign policy. Do something useful with your anger. I can strip furniture with a displeased glance, for instance.

Gold Feathers

An impoverished child nursed a magical, injured swan back to health. In gratitude, the swan told the child to pluck one of its golden feathers and buy food with it. Everyone at the market marveled at the gold feather. A banker secretly followed the child home and discovered the golden swan. He grabbed the swan and brutally plucked its feathers, killing it. He went to the market and paid for everything with bloody clumps of gold feathers. Everyone could see that he had done something horrible and greedy, but they conducted business with him anyway because he was now very wealthy. This is how the financial services industry was born.

Vegetarian Discussion Question

Suppose you are a vegetarian. Unaware or for-getful of this fact, your dear, old auntie has labored mightily to cook and serve a glorious, golden, turkey dinner. If you eat some turkey, the subject of your pious vegetarianism will never be brought up in company, but you will feel that you have compromised yourself. If you refuse to eat any turkey, your auntie will be mortified, her feelings will be hurt, and the turkey will still be dead, but you will have hon-ored your principles.
Which is more humane? Hurting your auntie or eating turkey? Discuss.

NOVEMBER 25

For Lack of Gratitude

If you can't muster a shred of gratitude, it's suffi-cient to acknowledge that things could be worse. Perhaps that sounds pessimistic, but it's not. To a true pessimist, this is already the worst of all possible worlds, dominated by woe, unrelieved by joy. If you're capable of recognizing that things can get worse, you still have a glimmer of optimism. Milk it.

Gratitude

When you give thanks, who or what do you thank? If you were to thank everyone and everything deserving of thanks, you would never have a moment to be anything but grateful. Your acknowledgments would have to reach back to primordial slime and stardust, all the way up to your present-day intestinal microbes. Your existence depends upon a web of interrelationships without beginning or end. Most of us shoot a prayer to Big Roxy, like sending a greeting card. That's a nice gesture, as formal courtesies go, but it doesn't really cover it.

Superstitious Gratitude

Many people express gratitude as a kind of superstition. They fear that if they don't say thanks for what they have, it will be taken away by some omnipotent, punishing force. By offering thank-yous and hallelujahs, they hope to bend reality in their favor and remain in the good graces of some capricious universal monarch. It's strange, I think, that this all-knowing, all-powerful monarch can't see through selfish scheming.

Plants Have Feelings

Plants are intelligent and sensitive entities. They respond to their environment and tend to thrive with a little encouragement. They defend themselves against attack. They communicate with one another in subtle, startling ways. I sincerely doubt that a head of lettuce *wants* to be eaten by you any more than a turkey does. We best be as respectful as possible when raising and harvesting food, certainly. But don't kid yourself that you are more virtuous than others simply because of what you eat. Once you recognize that your existence relies on the extinguishment of countless other lives, maybe you'll actually do something of value rather than congratulate yourself for your superior ethical sensibility.

The Phantom City

Long ago, a small group of people made a difficult journey through the desert. They had traveled far. Their food and water were running low. They were giving up hope of ever reaching their destination. Suddenly, they saw a city in front of them. Safely inside its walls, they slept soundly for the first time in days. When they awoke, they found themselves again in the barren desert. The city had been an illusion. But the brief respite had given them heart to continue their journey. Illusion can be beneficial if it helps us cope with reality. But it's not a palatable substitute for reality. Much like vegan cheese.

The Ideal Is Not Real

Stop trying to change "what is" by ranting about "how it should be." Ideals are arbitrary standards of perfection to which idealists want us to conform. Ideals are conceptual prisons. Clean up your own mess. Do your best. Pay as you go. No other knowledge is purposeful. Why do you insist that the real world is broken? What if the world is exactly as it's supposed to be? There's a chilling thought.

Beyond Thinking

One of the most perceptive beings I ever knew was a dog. She wasn't particularly smart. She was always startled by the backyard motion detector turning the lights on when she went outside at night, for instance. But she was freakishly intuitive, attuned to the emotional states of people around her, and able to express devastatingly accurate commentary with a slight movement of her brow or turn of her head. There is more to intelligence than thinking, more to understanding than reason. Of course, when you are otherwise powerless and dependent on the whims of others, you develop uncanny abilities. Later in life, she frequently ate her own poop, but she was brilliant nonetheless.

Another Wronged Woman

A great shaman of the north once told me the story of Sedna, the sea goddess. She refused to marry any of her suitors and spent her days overeating. Thus, she was a burden on her father. So he paddled her out to sea and threw her out of the kayak. She tried to hold on, but her father chopped off her fingers, hands, and arms, which metamorphosed into the seals, fish, and other animals that populate northern waters. Sedna sank into the sea and became its queen. Ever since, hunters must assuage her if they want a bounteous kill. Folklore is full of horrifically wronged people who become rulers of worlds, and to whom others must make offerings to atone for primeval guilt. We are a troubled species.

Holiday Lights

Putting up a string of lights makes everything feel more festive. It requires very little work and makes the holiday season brighter. In the glow of my twinkling icicle display, I read the fine print on the packaging: Made in China by exploited children; may contain chemicals known by the State of California to cause cancer. Ho ho ho

Football Then and Now

When I was a girl, a football game was more genteel than a street brawl, and more innocent than the spectacle of Roman gladiators murdering each other in the ring. A game gave us an excuse to sit in the bitter cold, nip illicitly distilled corn whiskey, and shout silly slogans. Back then, football made aggression more sociable. Today, I'm afraid football makes aggression more socially acceptable. It is a game of violence, trash talk, and bad manners rewarded with acclaim and enormous sums of money. Just thinking about it makes me want to punch an offensive lineman.

Quell Animosity

So much needless animosity arises from people believing that you do not like them. People want to feel that they are liked. If they suspect that you dislike them, you will become their demon. As a general rule, do not broadcast your dislike. You don't have to like people. You don't have to make a show of pretending to like people. Just conceal your dislike as you would zip your fly if you suddenly noticed it to be open. This will save everyone a lot of embarrassment.

Bad Habits of the Enlightened

I spent months in a cave with a dazzling thousand-year-old, green-skinned meditation master named Brenda. She taught me how to levitate and make delicious tea out of nettles and mud. Many people don't realize that enlightened beings have irritating habits. Brenda would often imply that if I were enlightened, her quirks would no longer annoy me. No degree of attainment will allow me to tolerate billows of tobacco smoke blown in my face while I'm trying to bite my nails in peace.

DECEMBER 7

Getting Hammered

The Japanese have a saying: the nail that sticks up gets hammered down. Meaning, everyone is expected to share similar attitudes and opinions. Those who differ will be pounded into submission. Sadly, the phenomenon of social-control-via-cudgel is not confined to Japan. If you have a mind of your own, hardheadedness is a necessity.

DECEMBER 8

My Celebrity Crush

I once had a romantic crush on a mildly famous sports personality. Imagine my thrill when I boarded a red-eye from Honolulu and discovered that My Celebrity would be my seatmate for the entire eight-hour flight. We exchanged pleasantries. My Celebrity soon dozed off. I, however, could not sleep a wink, and not because my heart was throbbing. Rather, the fiery garlic breath of My Celebrity kept me wide-eyed and miserable the entire time. Reality is a sure cure for self-created infatuation.

The Way You Look at People

Please do one thing for me this holiday season: Change the way you look at people. Literally adjust your gaze. Soften it. Make it receptive. Right now, you look at others with impatience. You look at them the same way you look at your mobile device—expectant, demanding, and often frustrated to find no novelty or distraction. You peer impertinently. You evaluate ungenerously. Or you dodge eye contact all together. For once, use your gaze to welcome and receive like a warm, spiced, holiday beverage.

My Hypocrisy

I am a hypocrite. "Go for your dreams," I tell my students. "Follow your heart." Yet here I cling to the comforting stability of my job as a leading light of humanity. What I really want is to bake a decent loaf of bread. I should be mastering the art of ciabatta in Tuscany, yet here I am in the Rocky Mountains, where high altitude wreaks havoc on flour and yeast. Can anyone understand what a misery this is to me? A more troubling question—and one that has been with me longer: Why do I care what people understand, or don't, about me? More eggnog, please.

DECEMBER 11

Drive-By Analysis

I am delighted by your easy ability to talk with
anyone and your willingness to try anything.
Your warmth and humor create a sense of intimacy.
People feel as if they know you. But an important
part of you is hiding behind this persona. What you
hide is so tender it would open at the slightest
touch, and so huge it would expand like the sky.
The aching beauty of it scares you. It scares me, too.
We're just having cocktails. Keep it light.

Swamp Lotus Versus Bristlecone Pine

Some of my friends like to remind me that glorious lotus flowers bloom in mucky swamps. Meaning, a life mired in difficulties, defilements, and imponderables can nonetheless grow like the paradoxical lotus and become beautiful because of the ugliness that surrounds it. That's fine, but I prefer the analogy of the gnarled, weather-beaten bristlecone pine. Such a tree grows in dry soil and in relative isolation. Buffeted by wind and cold, it grows slowly and tenaciously. It doesn't shoot up like a swamp plant. It is perhaps the oldest living organism on earth, surviving for five thousand years and longer. It can serve as a landmark for generations. Think about that as you're traipsing through the woods looking for a Christmas tree to chop down.

Don't Expect an Apology

You will never receive the apology you feel you are owed. Perhaps the person who hurt you has no understanding of your distress or no feeling of remorse. In that case, an apology would be an empty formality. Also, it is possible that this person is so troubled or embarrassed by what has happened that he or she cannot even broach the subject with you. Face it. You're a difficult person to shop for. Offering a specific list of gift ideas might prevent a future *faux pas*. Don't make others try to read your mind.

Thoughts on Giving

As you shop for holiday gifts, keep in mind the true spirit of giving. Obviously, you should give with no thought of receiving anything in return. But you can't help it. You always think of what you will receive, if only the satisfaction of having given well. In the true spirit of giving, there is no giver, no recipient and no object given. Meaning, you recognize no distinction or separation between you and the other person; the giver, recipient, and gift are one and the same. When you give in this spirit, the gift represents your deep, interdependent relationship with the other. This is what I mean when I give you soap.

Holiday Cookies

I once received by mail a tin of holiday cookies baked by a dear friend, an internationally acclaimed pastry chef. The cookies were shaped like festive holiday symbols, and were beautifully frosted. I eagerly popped one in my mouth. It was disgusting, absolutely vile. I began to worry about my friend's mental state. I wondered about my own. Still, I ate another cookie. By the time I had eaten a sixth, I knew I was eating pure genius—a symphony of lard, liver and indescribable tang. I called my friend to thank her. "They're a revelation," I gushed. She asked, "What does Razz think?" Turns out, they were intended as special treats for Razzle Muffin, my Bichon Frise. Put some effort into appreciating the gifts you receive. You may be surprised what you discover.

When You Are Dead

Can you accept that when you are dead the world will get along fine without you? One day all the people you have ever known will be dead. There will be no one to remember you. What then? What will your life have meant? Sorry to cut to the heart of existential angst during the holiday season, but we're running low on tomorrows.

Don't Pander

You want to be liked and appreciated, but that's not a suitable reason to cater to the base instincts of others. Do not aim low to win a cheap laugh. Express your vision, and give others a chance to rise to it. Do not pander to what is beneath you. Do not bring your whoopee cushion to grandma's party.

Your Deepest Desire

What is your deepest desire? To hurt others? To hurt yourself? I doubt it. I suspect that your deepest desire has something to do with love, joy, or redemption. Have the courage to want what you truly want. Don't judge what you want or push it away. Don't tell yourself it's possible or impossible. Don't speculate about what others might say. Don't alter your desire to make it seem more noble or selfless, or to make it reflect what you think you *should* want. Your thoughts, words, and deeds all grow from your deepest desire. They will grow strangely and bear problematic fruit if you're not honest with yourself about what you truly want.

The Problem of Craving

When I refer to desire, I'm talking about a feeling that fills you up. If you feel a lack—a needing or wanting to obtain something—you are in a state of craving or hunger, not desire. Hunger is a problem because it drives you to figure out a way to get what you want. You maneuver the object of your affection under the mistletoe, for example. You plot, plan, and rehearse lines of dialogue. You're manipulating the situation. Your rational thought process is screwing up everything. Just *desire*. Don't "do" anything other than that. Then you'll start to understand.

Admonitions against Scolding

Every religion with which I am familiar admonishes you not to scold, criticize, or find fault with your fellows. In criticizing, you are judging. You are implying that you are better than others. Some religions regard your judgments as usurpations of authority. Only God can judge; you must bite your tongue. Secular wisdom, too, warns that judging is somehow inherently injurious and unfair. It is no wonder, then, that you exercise spectacularly poor judgment. You're trained, as it were, to distrust your intuitive perceptions. You fear that your intuition is arbitrary, wrong, and at odds with divine judgment. Listen to your gut. It's rioting with information that you've dismissed for millennia.

Why Do You Love?

Why do you love the people you love? If you can state *reasons* for your love, I will be very sorry for you. Certainly, your loved ones have qualities that you value in particular, but your love is not contingent upon these qualities, is it? If so, I would argue that you do not love the person. Rather, you have a strategic or calculating relationship with him or her. If you love someone, you have to admit that you do not know why. You just intuitively know beyond a doubt that you love who you love. Love is completely irrational and intellectually indefensible yet wholly undeniable. So too is my belief in Santa Claus. Don't ruin it for me.

An Optimistic Turn

Relatively speaking, the winter solstice is the darkest day of the year. The depressive effects of gloom have been gaining on us all, I suspect. But today is also a turning point. A cycle is coming to an end, which means a new cycle is about to begin. Today we can say with assurance that tomorrow will be brighter, if only imperceptibly. This may not sound like much, but everything significant begins imperceptibly and grows by degrees, for good or ill. Today, at least, we're growing toward light.

You Have No Faith in Faith

A bunch of people found themselves in a pit from which they could not escape. A passerby threw down a long silk thread in hope of rescuing them. A man in the pit grabbed the thread and started to climb. Others warned that the thread would break and he would fall and die, but he kept climbing. You want a stout rope or sturdy ladder, but faith is an airy, thin thread. You feel you must build up your faith, bolster it with scripture and zeal. You don't believe that a delicate filament can hold you and everyone else. So you remain in the pit.

On Prayer

What are you doing when you pray? Are you beseeching the aid of a power beyond yourself? That's all very well. I do not beseech powers beyond myself because I know they are frantically busy with assignments from you. Yet I pray all the time. I am not praying to anyone or anything, so what am I doing? Bear with your auntie. I am old and weak, but my love and longing are stronger than ever. My desire does not come from another person or an external entity. It comes from within me. I feel that the "answer" must come from the same place. So I pray to fulfill my desire somehow from the inside. The disadvantage is that my miracles are personal glimmers rather than mass-market epics. But these days any miracle will suffice.

Follow Your Own Star

Everyone has an opinion about who you should be and what you should do with your life. It doesn't hurt to consider their advice, especially the advice of your dear auntie. But you have to make the journey on your own. No one else can do it for you. There are at least one hundred billion stars in the Milky Way Galaxy. Pick one out for yourself.

"Follow your own star"

Nostalgia

The day after a much-anticipated holiday or special occasion can feel like a letdown. It can evoke nostalgia. When I was a girl, nostalgia was a medical diagnosis of severe, debilitating homesickness. Back then, we pined so intensely that we emitted a pleasant fragrance of evergreen. One of my friends used to burn with such pensiveness he was like a sappy pinon log crackling on a fire, encircling us with sweet, enchanted smoke. We toasted marshmallows. Ah, I am nostalgic for the nostalgia of a bygone era. We can never return to the people, places, and circumstance of our past, which is why nostalgia is so painful but so pleasant.

DECEMBER 27

The Meaning of Life

The meaning of your life is intrinsic in your being alive. You don't need some external person or projection to speculate about what your life means. Work it out for yourself. One thing I will not tolerate, however, is your juvenile assertion that life is ultimately meaningless and you, therefore, are meaningless. This rips my heart open. You mean a great deal to me. You mean something to others, too, even if you don't think so. That's lesson one in discovering the meaning of life: it isn't just about you.

Spring Is Near

My backyard statue of St. Francis is buried under three feet of snow. I can see only the crown of his bald head. Looking at the silent, peaceful scene, I think of daffodil bulbs in the frozen ground. I think of dormant roots and bare, broken branches. If I hadn't seen my yard burst with greenery and life in the past, I would not believe it possible. I feel much the same when I look at you. Beset with hindrances, you seem unlikely to ever flower. But I know that you will bloom—as certainly as winter turns to spring. The new season will transform you in startling, beautiful ways. Meantime, be a dear and help me shovel my sidewalk. Spring is near. But let's not get ahead of ourselves.

DECEMBER 29

All Unions Are Bittersweet

You long to be close to others, but you fear it, too. You know that, eventually, you must part from everyone. You will fall out of love. Your friendships will rupture. Your job will be outsourced, and you will be displaced. The joy of union is always shadowed by the certainty of parting. Soon, you will miss my little sayings. But you will make your own, and they will fit you better.

A Day of Introspection

Metaphorically, I had lived much of my life thrashing on the surface of a rough sea. It wore me out. So I stopped and allowed myself to sink. Now the currents carry me, effortless. Everything is liquid and luminous. I hope to go deeper, down to the darkness where not even the sun can go, where strange beings generate their own light and warmth rises from the heart of earth. Let's go. Let's make a day of it. Then we can rocket to the surface, take a great gulp of air and go for sushi.

A Strong Finish
Is a Bold Beginning

Today you cross from one year into the next. You step out of the cave of my tutelage and onto your own meandering path. It's like leaving a movie theater and walking out into the bright sunshine. Everything is suddenly more vivid and glaring. You have to blink and think about where to go next. Somehow, you're going to transform yourself. Improve yourself. Never has your resolve been stronger.